A GUIDE TO THE
CIVIC HERALDRY
OF ENGLAND
UP TO THE
FIRST WORLD WAR

A GUIDE TO THE CIVIC HERALDRY OF ENGLAND

UP TO THE FIRST WORLD WAR

by Ray Westlake

The Naval & Military Press

For Angharad Ellis
who brightens my day

© Ray Westlake 2019

Published by

The Naval & Military Press Ltd
Unit 5 Riverside
Bellbrook Industrial Estate
Uckfield, East Sussex
TN22 1QQ England

Tel: +44 (0) 1825 749494
www.naval-military-press.com

CONTENTS

Acknowledgements ix

Introduction xi

Civic Arms 1

A Guide to the Civic Heraldry up to the First World War 3

Bibliography 110

ACKNOWLEDGEMENTS

Many important books have been used during the research for this, the first in a series of 'Guides' to heraldry. However, I must give special thanks to the following writers for the inspiration that their works have given me: A. C. Fox-Davies, Gale Pedrick and C. Wilfrid Scott-Giles. In modern times, several websites dealing with heraldry compiled by councils and local historians have been most helpful, but I must make specific mention of **civicheraldry.co.uk** (Robert Young) and **heraldry-wiki.com** and thank their owners for the tremendous amount of dedicated hard work that they have carried out. It could be said that without the sources mentioned above this book would not have been possible; without them, it would certainly have taken many years longer to write. But essential to any writer is the support and encouragement from his or her partner. In my case, my wonderful wife Claire who knows about commas and colons and, more to the point, where they should or should not go.

INTRODUCTION

As the medieval knight closed the visor of his helmet he immediately rendered himself anonymous. He was in battle and, well-armed as he may have been, he may not survive unless he knew who his friends, as well as enemies, were. He needed to be recognised. Clearly seen among his weapons was his shield and it was upon this that his emblem (his charge) was placed. Surcoats would be decorated, giving us the term 'coat of arms', as was horse furniture, flags and pennants. Emblem, insignia or badge, this was by far the better way to recognise someone from a distance than letters. The simple soldier could not read, anyway. Despite the wars of ancient times being long past, soldiers fighting in twentieth-century wars were still being recognised by their insignia. I can think of numerous incidents recalled in the memories of men who fought in the war of 1914-1918 of how, lost in the confusion of battle, they found their unit by the cap badges of the dead.

I have heard the words 'that's us' many times, but the most memorable must be on the occasion that my father and I passed the image of a Royal Artillery gun badge set into a wall. The 'that's us' referred to the fact that Dad had served in the Royal Artillery during the Second World War. He was a 'Gunner', and proud of it. The 'us', in this case, represented pride of regiment. Along the same lines, I hear the comment coming from my own lips when passing the Royal Fusiliers Memorial in Holborn, the short service as a cadet with that regiment having had a welcome and lasting effect. 'That's us', certainly, whenever I see that flaming grenade insignia worn in the berets of old soldiers parading some November morning in London or elsewhere.

Businessmen do the same when, finger pointing, they show a trademark or logo. It would be similar in the case of a football or cricket club supporter, someone seeing the arms or badge of their school, country, city or town. Be it coat of arms, badge, insignia, sign, symbol, trademark or logo, this is heraldry and a quartered shield, crest or set of supporters will often do much to open their stories.

Richmond Herald of Arms, J. P. Brooke-Little refers to the 'science' of heraldry. Certainly, it is a serious subject requiring, in every aspect, correct form. It has its own language.

The delight of all heraldry is how each seal, coat of arms or badge can be seen as a journey through its owner's history. With this in mind I have researched each entry and tried to arrive at the reasons why the several devices have been used. I cannot claim completeness in this as many of these origins have been lost in time, if indeed they ever existed.

This is the first in a series of 'Guide' books dealing with non-personal arms and badges. Following will be a volume covering the civic heraldry of Scotland, Wales and Ireland. Also planned are books on universities, schools, societies, institutes, guilds, clubs and businesses. The armed services, of course, have heraldry too and another volume will tackle the vast subject of badges belonging to Britain's Navy, Army and Air Force.

CIVIC ARMS

We see them all about in stone, metal and wood. There above town hall entrances, on library walls, law courts and on gates to refuge departments. Crematoriums have them, so do park keepers' huts, the sides of buses, dustcarts and offices of weights and measures. Caretakers in council flats have them on their hats. They come in paper, too. Rate demands have them; so do letters from the mayor's parlour which, before 'cut backs' possibly, were embossed on fine paper. From these lions, stags, fierce bulls, wolves with chains around their necks, dogs with collars, beasts, real and mythical, look down on us. To the dexter and sinister, steadfast they perch on heraldic wreaths alongside mottos inscribed on ornate scrolls. In sable, vert, gules and azure: wheat sheaves, scallop shells, fleurs-de-lis, bishops' mitres, open books showing learning, wheels and cogs for industry adorn the shields (whole, divided or quartered) which they guard. Civic coats of arms, some ancient and 'official', some the whim, perhaps, of a past mayor. Their records of adoption long lost and, if ever written down, now hidden among the dusty minute books and archives of local authorities.

'The use of armorial bearings by local authorities', notes C. Wilfrid Scott-Giles, MA, in his authoritative book *Civic Heraldry of England and Wales*, 'is traceable to the practice of authenticating documents by means of official or corporate seals...' Early use of these seals can be traced back to the latter part of the twelfth century. It was soon found that simple and inexpensive designs left the doorway open for the forger, fake documents bearing so-called 'official' authorisation being offered as a means to gaining trade orders. More intricate designs were therefore required, a practice still in use today in the production of bank notes. Most early town seals used emblems associating the place with: royalty, lords of manors, benefactors, religious devices borne by the town's patron saint, castles indicating strength, images associated with local trade or ships by those with strong maritime connections. Armorial bearings (coats of arms) soon followed, with many of the devices previously used on seals finding their way onto the new coat. Some, however, were too intricate and many did not conform with heraldic custom and had to be omitted or modified.

Following is an alphabetical listing of the several English counties, cities and towns that were in possession (official or otherwise) of seals or arms by the end of the First World War. No claim of completeness can be offered, but it is a hoped that this 'Guide' will encourage further research into the fascinating subject of heraldry.

A GUIDE TO THE CIVIC HERALDRY OF ENGLAND UP TO THE FIRST WORLD WAR

ABINGDON (Berkshire)

Five crosses on a green ground, one large in gold and four of the silver pattée type. This design was recorded by the Heralds in 1556 and, notes C Wilfrid Scott-Giles, may have been based on that of Abingdon Abbey which dates from AD 675. The central cross is in reference to Christ, the others recalling the four Evangelists. Illustration from the 1894 edition of *The Book of Public Arms*.

ABRAM (Lancashire)

The seal has a tower with three turrets between two suns. Situated on the northeast bank of the Leeds and Liverpool Canal, Abram anciently formed a township within the parish of Wigan which features a tower of three turrets in its arms.

ACCRINGTON (Lancashire)

Seen on the arms is a textile shuttle, two printing cylinders and a piece of calico cloth, all representations of Accrington's industries. Note how the crest takes the form of a leafy branch of oak bent to form the letter 'A'. The Hargreaves family of Broad Oak were connected with cloth mills in the area, the stag being from their arms, the lion being from those of the De Lacy family who held Accrington by grant of Henry II. The arms were granted 26 August 1879. Illustration from an Edwardian postcard.

ALCESTER (Warwickshire)

Prior to a grant of arms in March 1955, Alcester Rural District Council used a seal which incorporated a crown.

ALDEBURGH (Suffolk)

A C Fox-Davies in both editions of *The Book of Public Arms* records that Aldeburgh has no armorial bearings, but a seal was granted on 20 October 1561 comprising a ship of three masts in full sail at sea, the mainsail charged with a lion rampant. No details of colours are given. The seal was, however, recognised as a coat of arms with the specified colours of blue sky, red lion in 1951. Situated on the North Sea coast, Aldeburgh was once a sizable port.

ALDERSHOT (Hampshire)

A C Fox-Davies states in both editions of *The Book of Public Arms* that Aldershot has no armorial bearings, but arms have been attributed to it in the form of an alder tree and three heaps of shot. A skilful play on words for the 'Home of the British Army' since the 1850s. An Edwardian postcard is illustrated.

ALDRIDGE (Staffordshire)

The town's device consists of a beacon which is reference to Bar Beacon, a local landmark.

ALNWICK (Northumberland)

The parish church of St Michael the Archangel at Alnwick dates from the fifteenth century and it is the figure of the saint destroying the dragon that appeared on the town's seal. The arms of Northumberland County Council include a representation of the Alnwick seal. Illustration from *Borough Seals of the Gothic Period* by Gale Pedrick.

ALTRINGHAM (Cheshire)

The arms of the town are shown and described in both editions of *The Book of Public Arms* as being a red and gold shield, the only charge being a silver lion in the first quarter. A C Fox-Davies suggests in his text that these are the arms of the Cheshire family of Massy.

ANDOVER (Hampshire)

It is said that the lion and tree depicted in the Andover seal are in reference to the old royal hunting lodge once found in the area. A C Fox-Davies provides no details of colours, but Burke's *General Armoury*, which refers to the shield as a coat of arms, gives the lion as gold.

APPLEBY (Westmorland)

In the illustration we see, serving as a crest, the salamander engulfed by flames. Lizard-like, with a slender body, blunt snout and short limbs projecting at right angles to the body, the salamander is reputed to be able to withstand fire, the reference here being that Appleby held out against numerous attacks by the Scots—especially that of 1388 when the place was sacked. Rightfully too, Appleby boasts in its motto '*Nec ferro nec icni*' (Neither by sword nor fire).

Also associated with fire, but they look peaceful here, are the two red dragon supporters which recall the ancient British Kingdom of Cumbria. The three lions, certainly based on the Royal Arms of England, are no strangers to the town as they appeared in the thirteenth-century seal of Appleby Corporation which also displayed apple trees. They are said to recall that King John gave the borough to the burgesses.

ARUNDEL (Sussex)

An old seal of Arundel displays a swallow in flight. The swallow, which has the scientific name of *hirondelle,* is an allusion to the place name. No mention of colours is made in either edition of *The Book of Public Arms,* but Burke's *General Armoury* gives the bird as black. Illustration from an Edwardian postcard.

ASHBURTON (Devonshire)

The seal of Ashburton dates from the fourteenth century and features a representation of the chapel of the Chantry of St Lawrence, founded in 1314 by Bishop Stapleton of Exeter. There is also a teazle, remembering the town's woollen industry, a saltire cross for St Andrew's Church in West Street, a shining sun and crescent moon. The sun and moon, according to Gales Pedrick in his book *Borough Seals,* are old Phoenician emblems and are to signify the Stannary rights of tin mine workers. Ashburton was once an important centre for the administration of the tin industry.

ASHFORD (Kent)

The old South Eastern Railway once repaired its locomotives at New Cross in London, but a larger site was needed and the company set up new works at Ashford in Kent. By 1850 some 130 houses for workers had been built, the population in 1882 being recorded as around 1300. The importance of the railway is represented in the arms illustrated by an early 0-6-0 locomotive. An uncomplicated design formulated by the Council Surveyor around 1860, seen also in the arms is the White Horse of Kent and three black circles from the Fogge family, a member of which was responsible for the building of the town's church—the thirteenth-century St Mary's. But some say that the circles could represent the tops of barrels in allusion to the Kent hop trade.

ASHTON-IN-MAKERFIELD (Lancashire)

The town makes use of the insignia of the baronetcy of Gerard, a silver shield charged with a red saltire cross and the red hand device of a baronet. A lion rampant forms the crest and a motto '*En Dieu est mon esperance*' translates as My hope is in God.

ASHTON-UNDER-LYNE (Lancashire)

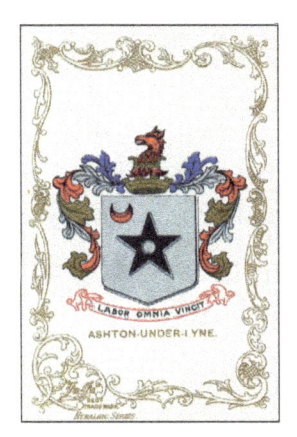

This town had no arms, records A C Fox-Davies in both his 1894 and 1915 editions of *The Book of Public Arms* but used in part those of the family of Ashton: a black mullet star and red crescent moon on the shield, and a griffin as a crest. An official grant, however, was made on 7 July 1926. Illustration from an Edwardian postcard.

ASTON MANOR (Warwickshire)

Happily munching a juicy nut, a squirrel enclosed within a silver circle serves as the crest to the arms granted to Aston Manor on 22 March 1904. The shield is divided into four quarters, two having three pattée crosses, two each with a pair of lions. A local government to the north of Birmingham, Aston Manor became incorporated into the County Borough of Birmingham in 1911. Illustration from the 1915 edition of *The Book of Public Arms.*

ATHERTON (Lancashire)

The town made use of the arms belonging to the second Baron Lilford who in 1797 married the heiress of the Atherton family—Henrietta Maria Atherton. In doing so he incorporated her arms (three sparrowhawks and a blue swan) into his own (a lion's forepaw and two crosses). Baron Lilford's family name was Powys. Illustration from the 1915 edition of *The Book of Public Arms*.

AUDENSHAW (Lancashire)

The red and white roses indicate the town's location close to the boundary between Lancashire and Yorkshire, the pick and waterwheel representing local industries. Audenshaw had expanded after the Industrial Revolution as an important centre for textile manufacture. The star (a spur-rowel) is in reference to former Lords of the Manor, the Assheton family from whose arms it comes.

AXBRIDGE (Somersetshire)

This small town lies on the River Axe close to the Mendip Hills and has as its seal a Paschal Lamb. Illustration from the 1894 edition of *The Book of Public Arms*.

AYLESBURY (Buckinghamshire)

Both editions of *The Book of Public Arms* state that Aylesbury has no armorial bearings. There is, however, an Edwardian Falkner postcard which shows a swan.

BACUP (Lancashire)

Granted in 1883, the arms of Bacup indicate much of the town's trade. Here we have a fleece, bales of cotton and a block of stone complete with a lewis attached (that essential stonemasons' tool) and, representing industry in general, two bees. The squirrel and stag are reminders of the ancient forest of Rossendale. Illustration from an Edwardian Ja-Ja postcard.

BANBURY (Oxfordshire)

An early seal for the town shows the branch of a tree with flowers and fruit and the letters B and A. The 1894 edition of *The Book of Public Arms* illustrates what the author refers to as the 'present seal'—a gold sun in splendour on a blue field and the motto *'Dominus nobis sol & scutum'* (The Lord is our sun and shield).

BARNARD CASTLE (Durham)

Not mentioned in either editions of *The Book of Public Arms* (1894 and 1915), but a Ja-Ja postcard of 1905 shows the town seal as a cross between a crescent and a star.

BARNET (Hertfordshire)

The Battle of Barnet was fought on 14 April 1471 between Edward IV and Richard

Neville, Earl of Warwick during the Wars of the Roses. The crossed swords in the arms adopted by the urban district council recall the event, the outcome of which it is said was due to the confusion of the two rose badges. C Wilfrid Scott-Giles notes that the flames refer to the supposed derivation of the name Barnet which means place of burning. The hart, of course, is from the arms of the county.

BARNSLEY (Yorkshire)

Much of this Yorkshire town's history and the people and industries associated with it is depicted in its shield, crest and supporters. Granted in 1869 (arms and crest) and 1913 (supporters), they show shuttles and pickaxes representing cloth and coal production. The local families of Locke, Beckett and Wentworth are represented by a falcon grasping a padlock, boars' heads and a griffin respectively, while the cups and cross in the upper section are from Monk Bretton Priory in close by Lundwood and dating from 1157. Another shuttle, this time on a shield, forms part of the crest and is displayed in the care of Mr Wentworth's griffin. In the supporters we have a miner, complete with pickaxe and lamp, and yet another of Barnsley's trades, glassblowing. Mining, cloth and glass—*'Spectemur agendo'* (Let us be judged by our works). Illustrations from the 1915 edition of *The Book of Public Arms* and a Wills's cigarette card which omits the supporters.

BARNSTAPLE (Devonshire)

The castle at Barnstaple was built by Juhell of Totnes while William the Conqueror was on the throne. Here it is, silver on a red background. Gale Pedrick, in his book *Borough Seals,* illustrates a seal showing part of Barnstaple's sixteen-arched bridge over the River Taw. Here too is a representation of St Thomas's Chapel, which once stood on the south-eastern side of the river, and a stone cross which stood at the western entrance to the bridge where money was collected to pay for maintenance. The eagle on the seal was once used as a device by the borough, as seen in the Debrett's *House of Commons* illustration.

BARROW-IN-FURNESS (Lancashire)

The bee and arrow placed on the shield are there as a rebus of the town's name—B-arrow. The former also represents the industry brought to Barrow during the nineteenth century by, in the main, the Duke of Devonshire, Duke of Buccleugh and Sir James Ramsden who was the first mayor and the main landowner of the area. The three respectively are represented by the serpent, stag and ram's head (another play on words) in the arms. The ship seen in the top section of the shield reminds us that Barrow was a major shipbuilding centre. Illustration from the 1915 edition of *The Book of Public Arms*.

BASINGSTOKE (Hampshire)

In the seal of Basingstoke we see the Archangel Michael armed with sword and spear while standing over the body of a dragon, the spear having thrust through its neck. Towards the northern end of Church Street the in-most-part sixteenth-century parish church at Basingstoke, is St Michael's. Illustrations from the 1894 edition of *The Book of Public Arms* and an Edwardian postcard.

BATH (Somersetshire)

This popular tourist attraction has a plain shield for its authorised arms displaying a sword in front of a battlemented stone wall and wavy lines representing water. The sword (that of St Paul) is in reference to the Bath Abbey, which is dedicated to St Peter and St Paul. The wall and water remember the Roman baths that bring so many to the city. The shield is often shown together with a lion and bear as supporters and a coronet crest. Illustrations are from the 1915 edition of *The Book of Public Arms* and a c1905 Ja-Ja postcard.

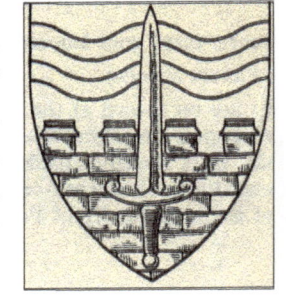

BATLEY (Yorkshire)

Perched above the arms of the town sits a dove holding an olive branch in its beak. On the shield below is a red chevron charged with three stars a fleece and wheatsheaf which refer to local industries. The main occupations of the town were farming and weaving, its first water powered mill for carding and spinning reaching Batley in 1796. The production of Shoddy, the name given to the recycling of old clothing into blankets and carpets, saw many employed in more than thirty mills. Below the chevron is the black cross belonging to the Copley family who could be found at Batley Hall.

BATTERSEA (London)

Simplicity itself are the arms of this London borough. Adopted after the passing of the London Government Act of 1899 from an old flag of Battersea dating back to 1803, a plain shield is divided into two colours, one half sky blue, the other silver. There is a crest of a dove holding in its beak an olive branch and a Latin motto which translates as 'Neither for myself, nor yourself, but for us'. Illustrations are from a 1905 Wills's cigarette card and the 1915 edition of *The Book of Public Arms*.

BECCLES (Suffolk)

Arthur Charles Fox-Davies points out in his 1894 edition of *The Book of Public Arms* that this town had no arms and illustrates a seal showing a church-like building with the motto '*Sigillum council municip Becclesiæ*' and the date 1836. The date refers to the Municipal Corporations Act of that year. Beccles is dominated by the detached, sixteenth-century perpendicular Gothic-in-style bell tower of St Michael's Church.

BEDFORD (Bedfordshire)

Placed firmly on the breast of a black eagle is a representation of the castle once the stronghold of the Beauchamps, the ancient barons of Bedford. The eagle too is from that family's heraldry. William de Beauchamp is noted for his part in the First Barons' War of 1215 and frequently entertained the 'rebellious barons' at his Bedford Castle seat, hospitality that saw him excommunicated by Pope Innocent III. The illustrations are from the 1894 edition of *The Book of Public Arms* and *Borough Seals* by Gale Pedrick.

BEDFORDSHIRE

The 1894 edition of *The Book of Public Arms* shows the seal of the county council with its tree, plough, garb and sheers. The 1899 edition of Cassell's *Gazetteer of Great Britain and Ireland* referes to the county's Dunstable and Luton Downs upon which 'are sheep walks, and they yield useful chalk manure for the lower lands.' Excellent corn is produced, the farms being noted as generally small.

BEDWORTH (Warwickshire)

The seal of Bedworth Urban District Council prior to arms being granted in 1969 shows a shield charged with eight mullets, a six-pointed star and the words 'We grow by industry'. The shield, notes Chris J Smith, was based on the arms of Nicholas Chamberlaine, Rector of Bedworth 1663-1715. He had given much of his lands to Bedworth and had established almshouses and schools in the town. The 1899 edition of Cassell's *Gazetteer of Great Britain and Ireland* notes Bedworth's local industries as coal and ironstone mines and the manufacture of hats, tape and ribbons.

BELPER (Derbyshire)

C Wilfrid Scott-Giles records a seal which bears the ancient arms of England and France (lions and fleur-de-lis) and believes that these are in reference to John of Gaunt, military leader, statesman and the third son of Edward III of England, of whom it is said once resided at Belper.

BERKHAMPSTEAD (Hertfordshire)

The arms show a three-towered castle, the two outer towers flying banners charged with red crosses, and sixteen roundels. Berkhamsted's castle is of Norman origin, the roundels having a connection with the Dutchy of Cornwall and Edward, the Black Prince. Records show that Berkhamsted Castle was a favourite residence of royalty and historic figures such as Thomas Becket and Geoffrey Chaucer.

BERKSHIRE

Both editions of *The Book of Public Arms* point out that the county had no armorial bearings but refers to 'a coloured sheet of the Arms of the Counties of England and Wales, which has been published' that give five silver heads on a red ground as Berkshire's arms. A C Fox-Davies makes the observation that 'this is evidently a perversion of the Seal and Arms of Reading.' But the device of a stag and oak tree has been associated with the county for centuries and was in fact mentioned by the Elizabethan poet Michael Drayton (1563-1631) in his account of the Battle of Agincourt. A valuable early heraldic reference, we read in the poem of the devices displayed on the several banners as the armies took the field: '...The Devonshire Band, a Beacon set on fire, Somerset a Virgin bathing in a Spring...Wiltshire a Crowned Pyramid...Berkshire a Stag, under an Oak that stood....' The Royal Berkshire Militia wore the badge, and this was taken into use by the regular and volunteer battalions of the Royal Berkshire Regiment in 1881. A glengarry badge of the 1st Volunteer Battalion is illustrated and a group of regimental badges that includes an officer's Victorian helmet plate (photo courtesy of Bruce Bassett Powell/Bob Bennett/Uniformology.com).

BERMONDSEY (London)

When the Danes occupied a camp at Southwark, Ethelred called upon the Norwegian King Olaf Haraldsson to help clear the invaders from the Thames. A successful attack was made on London Bridge with a fleet of ships, Olaf then going on to retake London. Beaten, off home went the Danes in April 1014. Here in Bermondsey's arms we see a crown and battle-axe, both emblems of the Saint King Olaf. He was also remembered by a Church of St Olaf (demolished after being deemed redundant in 1926) in Tooley Street. The lion and crozier are in reference to the ancient Abbey of Bermondsey, which was founded as a monastery by wealthy Londoner Aylwin Childe, and the ship recalls Bermondsey's centuries-old activities in the shipbuilding industry. A three-masted battleship formed part of the old seal of Rotherhithe Vestry, Rotherhithe recorded in the Domesday Book as being included in the Royal Manor of Bermondsey. 'Arts benefit the people' exclaims the motto. Bermondsey's arms were granted in March 1901. Illustration from the 1915 edition of *The Book of Public Arms*.

BERWICK-UPON-TWEED (Northumberland)

The town's seal provides an insight into much of Berwick-upon-Tweed's history. The regal figure at the top of the design is thought by some authorities to be a representation of Edward III to whom the town surrendered after his victory at close-by Hallidown Hill in 1333. But the two Royal Arms shields that we see are of a type that post-dated Edward's reign. Possibly, notes C Wilfrid Scott-Giles, the seated figure is a representation of some Lancastrian or Yorkist monarch. The bear and tree (a wych-elm) are a rebus on the town's name. Illustrations are from the 1894 edition of *The Book of Public Arms* and an Edwardian postcard.

BETHNAL GREEN (London)

Not mentioned at all in the 1894 edition of *The Book of Public Arms* and only as 'Has no arms' in 1915. 'The Beggar's Daughter of Bethnal Green' is a long poem which appeared in Thomas Percy's *Reliques of Ancient English Poetry* of 1765. The beggar was blind and was, in fact, Henry de Montfort who met his end at the Battle of Evesham on 4 August 1265. Legend has it, however, that he escaped death and was rescued by a young girl, the daughter of one of the barons beside whom he had fought. But he was ashamed of his part in the battle and, having married the girl, assumed the identity of a blind beggar. A daughter was later born, and it is she who we see in the Bethnal Green seal taking a leisurely walk with her blind father. The badge illustrated was worn in civilian jackets by members of a First World War home defence unit formed at Bethnal Green.

BEVERLEY (Yorkshire)

From an old town seal came the beaver and wavy lines representing water, an obvious play on the town's name. A beaver is often used in heraldry to indicate industry, those in Beverley in 1899 being noted as tanning, foundries, chemical production and an important corn trade. Gale Pedrick, in his book of borough seals, mentions a seal which featured the seated figure of St John of Beverly lifting up his right hand in benediction. He is credited as being the founder of Beverley having built the town's first structure: a monastery. St John's Catholic Church in the town bears his name.

BEWDLEY (Worcestershire)

Bewdley was once a busy inland port connected to the sea by the River Seven and we are reminded of this by the anchor in its arms. The old quayside has long ago been overgrown by housing and other buildings. Other devices are connected with Edward IV, the manor of Bewdley having been assigned to the Crown upon his accession. Illustration from the 1894 edition of *The Book of Public Arms*.

BEXHILL-ON-SEA (Sussex)

The several Martello towers built along the Sussex coast for defence have long been claimed by the sea, destroyed or demolished. But as such a feature of the area the town chose to include one of them as a crest in its coat of arms. Bexhill also remembers in its achievement (granted 21 January 1907) the mitre of the Bishops of Chichester, who owned the manor from the time of the Conquest until Henry VIII came to the throne, and also the Earl De La Warr who included a star within his crest. Seen too are the half lion, half ship's hull from the Cinque Ports device, the mallard from Mayor of the Borough from 1907 to 1908, the Earl of Brassey and the sun and sea that represent Bexhill's reputation as a popular seaside and health resort. The transformation of Bexhill into a resort was due to an idea of the 7th Earl de la Warr who gave the building work to John Webb. The birds (martlets) decorating the border are a feature of Sussex and other towns of the county.

BIDEFORD (Devonshire)

The seal illustrated in the 1894 edition of *The Book of Public Arms* shows a one-arched bridge over a river and, passing through it, a single-masted ship. Could this be remembering the exploits of Sir Richard Grenville and men from Devon in the *Revenge* during the Battle of Flores in 1591? Grenville was from Bideford, born in the manor house on Bridge Street, who built a new mansion on the quayside in 1585. He was responsible for the creation of a port at Bideford which specialised in tobacco importation from America. One of the longest medieval bridges in England is the twenty-four-arched Bideford bridge which crosses the River Torridge and links the old part of the town with the new.

BILSTON (Staffordshire)

Bilston Urban District Council was not granted arms until September 1933 but took into use prior to that a device based on the heraldry of Sir Walter de Bilston, a local landowner who, it is said, fought at the Battle of Evesham in 1265: three silver martlets on a black bar and a Stafford knot.

BINGLEY (Yorkshire)

C Wilfrid Scott-Giles records that Bingley Urban District Council had made use of the Bingley family arms which show three black trefoils and a silver bear's head.

BIRKENHEAD (Cheshire)

The principle devices incorporated into the Birkenhead arms (granted 28 August 1878) had been taken from seals belonging to various local bodies within the borough. In the 1949 Paxton Chadwick depiction of the arms illustrated, we see the pastoral staff and lion from the seal of Birkenhead itself, while the oak tree on a green mound comes from the Tranmere Local Board. John N C Lewis, in his book *The Arms of Cheshire,* tells how Cannon Tarver of Chester suggested the motto which translates as 'Wherever there is faith here is also light and strength'. The cannon links this with the several charges included in the arms: The cross and pastoral staff suggesting faith, the star and crescent, light and the oak and lions, strength.

BIRMINGHAM (Warwickshire)

It is the arms of the De Bermingham family, holders of the manor in the thirteenth century and possible before, that appear on the shield of those granted to Birmingham in 1889. Think of the 'Second City', and you think of numerous important industries, Birmingham for many years a centre for the manufacture of guns, for one. We are reminded of this by the left supporter, with his hammer and anvil, the right arm issuing from the mural crown of the crest. The city is also proud of its arts and we see this recognised by the figure of a women holding an artist's palette and brushes while serving as the right supporter. Here at the town hall weekly recitals have been given since 1834, a triennial music festival being a feature of the city between 1784 and 1912. In the art world there was the Birmingham School, a group of landscape artists that originated in the 1760s, and it is the Birmingham Society of Art, for which we must thank the Birmingham Museum and Art Gallery. Illustrations: from the 1894 edition of *The Book of Public Arms*, an Edwardian postcard by Faulkner, and the crest used by the Royal Navy as a badge for HMS *Birmingham*.

BISHOP'S CASTLE (Shropshire)

The town seal has a domed castle with the letters I R for James Rex and the date 1609. According to one source it was King James I who, in 1609, gave the seal to Bishop's Castle when he confirmed the rights and privileges awarded by the 1573 Elizabeth I Great Charter. The castle was built to protect the town from the Welsh in 1087, the border between the two countries being just over a mile away. Illustration from the 1894 edition of *The Book of Public Arms*.

BISHOP'S STORTFORD (Hertfordshire)

The shield is divided into three vertical sections, two of green and a central one of silver upon which is charged a mitre and wheatsheaf, the former representing the Bishops of London, who were former landowners, and the latter, agriculture. Running across the shield are silver and blue wavy lines which allude to the River Stort and the ford from which the town takes its name. The crest, an embattled tower from which rises a red cross, is in reference to Bishop Stortford's ruined castle (Waytemore Castle) and St Michael's Parish Church. 'For God and people', translates the motto.

BLACKBURN (Lancashire)

The letter 'B' is, of course, the initial of this Lancashire town, but the three bees on the arms granted in 1852 are there to represent the skill, perseverance and industry of those who had brought Blackburn to be one of England's most productive industrial areas. Blackburn stands on the banks of the Blackwater which is represented by the central black wavy line. Here too is the bugle horn from the arms of W H Hornby, Blackburn's first mayor, the two diamond shapes (lozenges), the heraldic emblem for spinning, being from those of Lord of the Manor Joseph Feilden. Much wealth and employment arose from the town's mills, the dove and shuttle crest indicating this. Note how the dove, the emblem of peace, is linked to the shuttle by a length of thread. Blackburn's 140 mills were known world-wide for their production of both calico and a blue and white fabric known as 'Blackburn Check'.

BLACKPOOL (Lancashire)

In his 1894 edition of *The Book of Public Arms,* A C Fox-Davies seems far from happy, writing: 'It is difficult to know whether to be amused at the ludicrous idiocy of the "design" which has been assumed or amazed at the ignorance which has allowed such an abortion to be put into currency.' But nonetheless he includes an illustration which shows a shield displaying four seaside scenes: a pier with a small yacht approaching, five men in a rowing boat, a bathing hut and another, three-masted this time, ship. Enjoying the views, a swallow serves as a crest. Below the shield and on a scroll is the word 'Progress'. With this word in mind he ends his Blackpool entry with the following comment, 'Had the ribbon been made use of to label the foregoing concoction as "A present from Blackpool", it would have been a fitting sequence to the rest of the absurdity.' But all would have been well just five years after publication of the 1894 volume as, in 1899, new arms were granted for the offending Lancashire seaside resort.

Regularly filling the grooved slots in the track, sand and salt water did little to help the efficient running of Blackpool's tram system during the early days of its existence. But the service provided by the Blackpool Electric Tramway Corporation (formed in January 1884) has been a successful feature of this popular Lancashire seaside resort for more than a hundred years. So much so that the electrical system on which the trams ran was represented in the town's arms by a thunderbolt. Blackpool was, of course, a pioneer in the use of electricity for both traction and illumination. See it in the early postcard by Faulkner illustrated, centre top of the shield.

Doing much to increase the early population (less than 500 in 1801 to over 2,500 in 1851) thanks to their building programme, Henry Banks and his son-in-law John Cocker also hold prime positions. From their personal arms: a fleur-de-lis for Mr Banks, a lion rampant for his daughter's husband.

And, just flown in from the Irish Sea, a seagull crosses black and gold wavy lines—gold for Blackpool's miles of sandy beaches, and the black? Well, it's in the name. C Wilfrid Scott-Giles, in his *Civic Heraldry of England and Wales,* points out that in the crest it has been suggested that the sails of a windmill refer to 'the Fylde', a district in which Blackpool occupies a very important position—fylde being an old word meaning field. Once a feature of the area was its many windmills, some of which can be seen still. The one represented in Blackpool's coat of arms has a red rose of Lancaster in its centre. But in another suggestion from Mr Scott-Giles, could it be that in the sails of the windmill we simply have a reference to the health-giving breezes for which Blackpool is well known? The inclusion of the battlements of a tower is uncertain. The third illustration shows the town arms as they appeared on the cap badge of the 1st Battalion Blackpool Volunteers of 1914-1918.

BLANDFORD FORUM (Dorsetshire)

Illustrated is the town's seal which shows the Royal Arms of England between two ostrich feathers. The design also includes the letters D and L of which it is said stand for the Duchy of Lancaster, once the owners of the Manor of Blandford. Illustration from the 1894 edition of *The Book of Public Arms.*

BODMIN (Cornwall)

The town's seal shows a king seated under a canopy, crowned and holding in his right hand a sceptre. Illustration from the 1894 edition of *The Book of Public Arms*.

BOGNOR REGIS (Sussex)

In gold and blue, C Wilfrid Scott-Giles records that the arms illustrated were used by Bognor Regis Urban District Council, the left side of the shield being the arms of Sir Richard Hotham. In the eighteenth century, and with a view to draw the public to the town, Sir Richard made efforts to rename the place Hothampton. 'Hotham the Hatter' was a wealthy property developer and politician who had made his early fortune in the hat trade. The right side of the shield, with its five Cornish choughs, represents the arms assigned to the Kingdom of the South Saxons.

BOLTON (Lancashire)

The Bolton shield is divided by two gold strips (bendlets) which, it is said, represent a soldier's shoulder belt. Certainly the bolt seen in the top right corner is in memory of the well-known archer troops associated with Bolton. Serving a second purpose, the bolt also alludes to the first syllable of the name. To the right of the bolt, and representing Bolton's weaving industry, is a shuttle and next to this, a mule spinning spindle. The spinning mule machine much used throughout the mills of Lancashire was invented by Samuel Crompton, a native of Bolton. At the bottom, the red rose of Lancaster. Bolton was once within the Diocese of Mercia and the crest remembers this by the elephant from Coventry, the seat of the diocese. Note the mitre displayed on the elephant's side. As can be seen in the illustration (from *The Book of Public Arms,* 1894 edition) the elephant appears to be standing on an uneven surface. This is intentional and is to signify how Bolton (the town also has the name Bolton-le-Moors or Bolton-super-Moras) stands on a rocky moor.

BOOTLE (Lancashire)

Officially granted on 4 November 1869, we see in the arms three stags' heads, these from the Earls of Derby, three mural crowns from the Bootle family and three fleurs-de-lis which represent the Linacres of Yorkshire—the full name of the town is Bootle-cum-Linacre. The lighthouse crest indicates Bootle's position at the mouth of the River Mersey. It was the Mersey Docks and Harbour Board that built a lighthouse on the seawall at Bootle in 1877.

BOSNEY (Cornwall)

The seal of the town was described by Burke in his *General Armoury* as being a castle with three domed towers joined to each other by a circular wall. Mentioned in both editions of *The Book of Public Arms*, but not illustrated.

BOSTON (Lincolnshire)

In Boston's arms a ram sits comfortably on a woolpack while two mermaids support the shield. Important was the town's wool industry, as was its activity as a port. Note how each of the mermaids wears a crown. Scott-Giles in his *Civic Heraldry of England & Wales* refers to these, having received information from the town clerk, as representing the fact that two notable women in the reign of Henry VIII, Anne Boleyn and Princess Mary Duchess of Suffolk, were connected with Boston. More crowns, this time on the shield, which are said to represent the Dukes of Brittany, Richmond and Suffolk. Shown in Gale Pedrick's book on borough seals, is an old seal which features the full-length figure of a saint with a woolpack before him. He holds a pastoral staff in his right hand and a book in his left. Could this be St Botolph, to whom Boston's parish church is dedicated?

BOURNEMOUTH (Hampshire)

C Wilfrid Scott-Giles in his *Civic Heraldry of England and Wales* quotes an explanation of the town arms provided for him by Bournemouth Corporation. It seems that the area in which Bournemouth stands was once a Royal Demesne of King Edward the Confessor and it is much from his arms that we see on those of this popular seaside resort. The colours, blue and gold, are his, as is the cross and the six birds (martlets) seen in the top right-hand corner of the shield. But there are other thoughts. Martlets are also regarded locally as sand martins, representing Bournemouth's sand cliffs, while the colours and the fish suggest sky, sands and sea. During the Middle Ages the coast on which Bournemouth lies was constantly called to arms, the lion of England being in remembrance of that. The pine tree and roses crest all join up with the motto which translates as 'For beauty and salubrity'. Two illustrations: one from the 1894 edition of *The Book of Public Arms* another, a modern photograph of the arms on a park gate.

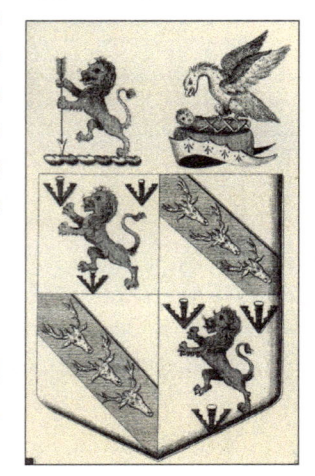

BRACKLEY (Northamptonshire)

Brackley has no arms of its own but uses a seal that bears those of the third Earl of Bridgewater who was Lord of the Manor during the seventeenth century. Illustration from the 1894 edition of *The Book of Public Arms*

BRADFORD (Yorkshire)

The arms illustrated are from an Edwardian postcard and represent a good likeness of those authorised in 1847 and used prior to 1907. When John of Gaunt passed lands to John Northrop of Manningham as a thank you for slaying the boar that had been terrifying Cliffe Wood, he asked that there should be 'One blast with his horn upon St Martin's Day.' The service, which is performed in Bradford Marketplace, became a local custom and is remembered in the three bugle-horns shown on the shield. And what of the boar? He too is remembered by the crest. Look closely and you will see that the poor creature has been depicted without its tongue. Not an accident by the artist but alluding to the legend that when the boar was killed, the slayer cut out its tongue and presented it as evidence that the beast was no more. Remaining with the same story, the black object in the centre of the shield is, in fact, a representation of a well, a well being the place where the boar, as it made its daily visit to drink, was killed. 'Labour overcomes all things' reads the motto. Also illustrated is a badge once worn by the 3rd Yorkshire West Riding Rifle Volunteer Corps, which was formed in Bradford in 1859, in which the unfortunate boar makes another appearance.

BRENTFORD (Middlesex)

Both editions of *The Book of Public Arms* state that Brentford had not yet obtained arms. In his notes for Brentford and Chiswick C Wilfrid Scott-Giles mentions that Brentford Urban District Council had a seal which featured a representation of St Nicholas, to whom the parish church is dedicated.

BRIDGNORTH (Shropshire)

Although both editions of *The Book of Public Arms* include lengthy entries regarding the town's seal, neither offer an illustration. However, the arms shown on the 1909-dated postcard illustrated are based on the town's seal. With the shield of St George and the Royal Arms as company, we see a three-turreted castle which is representative of that built 1098-1101 by Robert de Belleme, later Earl of Shrewsbury. Parliamentary forces besieged the place in 1646, their three-week stay ending with the castle being reduced to ruins. Bridgnorth's Royalist loyalties are reflected in the town's motto, 'In the town's loyalty lies the King's safety'. A second illustration is from *Borough Seals* by Gale Pedrick.

17

BRIDGWATER (Somerset)

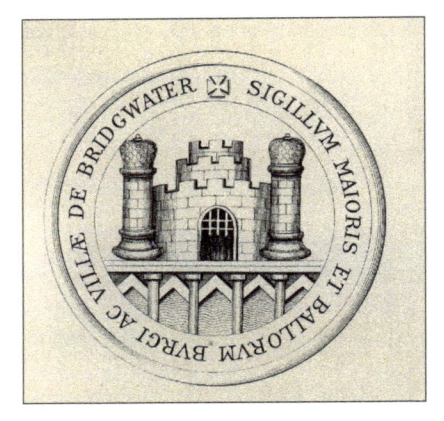

The town's seal dates from the fifteenth century and, with its image of a bridge over water, its meaning may seem obvious. But the water is not that of the River Parrett. Instead we have a corruption of Burgh Water, the borough of Walter de Douai, the Norman knight and major landowner in the South West of England. Standing on the bridge is the castle erected in the reign of Henry II by William de Briwere. The 1894 edition illustration from *The Book of Public Arms* shows the castle as having three towers, the central one being of a three-storied construction while the other two are domed. Also illustrated is a postcard dated 1907 which differs in that it has a single central tower and also includes a star and fleur-de-lis above the building.

BRIDLINGTON (Yorkshire)

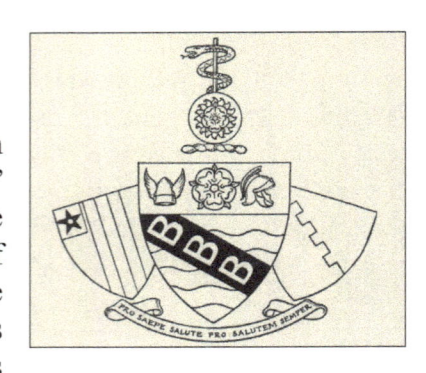

Illustrated is a detail from an Edwardian postcard by Ja-Ja which shows three 'Bs' across gold and blue wavy lines, the letters being from the arms of Bridlington Priory, the lines in reference to the Gypsey Race river which runs through the town. Bridport's history is recalled by the inclusion of Roman and Danish helmets, the white rose, of course, being for York. The Rod of Æsculapius in the crest is an emblem of health and is there to symbolize the importance of the town as a seaside resort and holiday centre. The motto recalls this and also tells how Bridport Bay has served as a refuge for shipping. The stone circle and its rose and sun insignia represent the Dyke Ring, the name of the wapentake in which the borough is situated. In his 1933 edition of *Civic Heraldry of England & Wales*, C Wilfrid Scott-Giles illustrates the same arms with the edition of shields belonging to two influential local families: the Hebblethwaites and Boyles.

BRIDPORT (Dorsetshire)

Bridport's shield is red with a silver castle above which are two gold fleur-de-lis and a gold lion. Silver and blue wavy lines representing water, the town is situated between the rivers Brit and Asker and was once a thriving port. For centuries Bridport was noted for its production of rope and the three gold objects seen in the open gateway were tools used in that trade. Bridport's arms were granted in September 1623. Illustration from the 1894 edition of *The Book of Public Arms*.

BRIERFIELD (Lancashire)

The coming of the Leeds and Liverpool Canal and the railway brought prosperity to the town during the early part of the nineteenth century. The first cotton mill was set up in 1832 at Lob Lane which was close to the Marsden coal pit. In the arms taken into use by Brierfield Urban District Council we have a silver chevron charged with two shuttles. At the bottom of the red shield a crossed shovel and pick and on the silver upper section, a spray of briar. C Wilfrid Scott-Gilles notes that in some representations of the arms the shovel and pick are replaced by a cock.

BRIGG (Lincolnshire)

For centuries the area now known as Brigg was used as a crossing point over the River Ancholme and was known as Glanford. When a bridge was built the name changed to Glanford Bridge which was then over the years shortened to Glanford Brigg and finally Brig. The seal of the town shows a bridge with the word 'Glamford' above.

BRIGHOUSE (Yorkshire)

Granted on 10 August 1893, the arms of Brighouse were based on those of the family of that name who had gold lions and black crescents. The crest, with its tiger's head, roses and embattles tower, are also courtesy of the Brighouse family. Illustration from the 1894 edition of *The Book of Public Arms*.

BRIGHTON (Sussex)

Birds (martlets) and dolphins, the former from the arms of Sussex, the latter an obvious choice for a town that has for so long depended on the sea, first as a fishing port, then as one of England's most famous pleasure resorts. Shown in the 1905 postcard illustrated are the arms as granted in 1897. 'We trust in God', reads the motto. Predating these by three years, the A C Fox-Davies 1894 illustration shows an earlier version.

BRISTOL (Gloucestershire)

The main charge of this city's arms shows a three-masted ship sailing out from a castle set upon a cliff. Banners, those of St George, fly from two domed towers. Bristol is, of course, well known for its connection with the sea and shipping. It was from Bristol that John Cabot set out on his several voyages of discovery, the port being the destination of ship-loads of tobacco for W D & H O Wills's cigarette factory and, unfortunately, slaves. The crest shows two bent arms rising from clouds, one hand grasping a snake, the other holding a pair of scales—a snake for wisdom, the scales representing justice. A pair of unicorns provide the supporters. Here, in the illustrations, we see the arms as depicted in an Edwardian postcard and the shield incorporated into one of the badges worn by the 1st Gloucestershire Rifle

Volunteer Corps, formed at Bristol in 1859. Also shown, and from Gale Pedrick's book *Borough Seals*, is the front and reverse of an old Bristol seal.

BRIXHAM (Devonshire)

The town's seal shows a representation of William, Prince of Orange landing at Brixham in 1688. He stands on the shore, raising his hat in one hand and with a drawn sword in the other. A ship at sea forms the background and a scroll bears the inscription 'Landing of the Prince of Orange, 1688'. The motto of the future William III, 'I will maintain', is also shown.

BROADSTAIRS AND ST PETERS (Kent)

Broadstairs (the name derives from the old steps that led from the sands up through the chalk cliffs to eleventh-century shrine of St Mary) became a popular seaside resort and soon earnt for itself the nickname of 'Star of the Sea'. And here we see it in the motto, part of the arms adopted by the urban district council. Here too are the half lions and half ships of the Cinque Ports, the white horse of Kent and a ship to remind us of the sea as an industry. The bird is usually described as a falcon, but could it be a seagull?

BROMLEY (Kent)

Arms for Bromley were granted in 1904. On the shield we see three black ravens in flight, two silver branches of broom, a representation of the sun, a scallop shell and a white horse. A skilful play on words here: the birds for the River Ravensbourne, upon which the town sits, the sun for the Manor of close-by Sundridge, broom for Bromley and the shell from the arms of the See of Rochester. The white horse is from the arms of Kent. Another shell and some broom for the crest and 'While I grow and hope' for the motto. Illustration from the 1915 edition of *The Book of Public Arms*.

BROMSGROVE (Worcestershire)

The seal has a boar within a wreath of oak. There is a medieval myth in which a small boy armed only with a wooden spear fought a boar in the forest that once stood around Bromsgrove.

BUCKINGHAM (Buckinghamshire)

The town's shield is divided black and red, the colours of the Staffords, Dukes of Buckingham. The white swan with a coronet around its neck is from the same source and is sometimes shown as chained. The illustration is from the 1894 edition of *The Book of Public Arms*.

BUCKINGHAMSHIRE

The County Council, notes C W Scott-Giles, has no arms but uses the white swan of the Staffords, Dukes of Buckingham. The illustration shows how it was used in the cap badge of the 1st Buckinghamshire Rifle Volunteer Corps which was formed in 1859.

20

BURFORD (Oxfordshire)

Regarding the drawing shown in the Visitation Books at the College of Arms of a lion rampant, A C Fox-Davies points out in his 1894 edition of *The Book of Public Arms* that 'it is difficult to say whether it be a seal or coat-of-arms.' His own illustration is shown.

BURNLEY (Lancashire)

The two black diamond shapes seen in the centre of the shield are known heraldically as fusils and were included, Scott-Giles explains, 'to symbolize the art of cotton spinning by which the town has attained its wealth and position.' Also in black is the lion at the bottom which comes from Henry de Lacy, once lord of the manor. Here too is an open hand representing bounty and liberality and is included 'to signify the extending of these qualities to the bees by which the industrious classes, the people, are represented' (Scott-Giles again). Bees are used in heraldry as symbols of industry, concord, peace, economy and people obedient to their rulers. The crane, which is used as a crest, is the emblem of vigilance. The motto translates as 'Both the prize and the motive of labour'. The first illustration is taken from the 1894 edition of *The Book of Public Arms*, the second is of a badge worn by the Burnley Volunteer Training Corps of 1914-1918.

BURSLEM (Staffordshire)

In 1759 the Ivy House in Burslem was leased to Josiah Wedgewood and it would be here that he produced beautiful pottery such as the Portland vases displayed in two quarters of the town's arms. Here too is a scythe, from the arms of the Sneyd family, and a silver fretted design courtesy of the Audleys. Another person associated with Burslem's history is Thomas Hulme, its first mayor, who is represented by the fleur-de-lis superimposed upon the garb crest. Born in August 1830, Thomas Hulme began as a clerk for John Wedgwood at the Woodland Street Works in Tunstall. Illustrations are from the 1915 edition of *The Book of Public Arms* and an Edwardian postcard. Burslem's arms were granted in 1878.

BURTON LATIMER (Northumberland)

The seal bears a Tudor rose. The name of the town is derived from the de Latimer family who occupied land there during the thirteenth century. Before this, it was called Burtone.

BURTON-UPON-TRENT (Staffordshire)

The top section of the arms illustrated in the 1894 edition of *The Book of Public Arms* shows two devices belonging to persons associated with the town, the eagle of the Paget family and the fleurs-de-lis courtesy of Mr M A Bass. The dissolution saw lands belonging to Burton Abbey awarded to the Pagets, while Mr Bass, who we must thank for his beers, founded the Bass Brewery from premises in Burton High Street in 1777. The fleurs-de-lis also has a connection to St Mary, to whom the abbey was dedicated. Silver and blue wavy lines represent the River Trent, the motto translating as 'Honour fosters the arts'.

BURY (Lancashire)

The arms granted in 1877 show a crest featuring a bee between two cotton flowers. Industrial is the bee, cotton being the town's leading industry. In the shield we see more of the same thing. Here is a golden fleece, a pair of shuttles, an anvil, this time for the iron industry, and three papyrus plants for paper making. 'Industry overcomes all things', reads the motto. Illustrated is the arms as shown in the 1894 edition of *The Book of Public Arms*. Debrett's *House of Commons* shows a shield charged with a chevron and three crosses which was in use prior to the 1877 grant.

BURY ST EDMUNDS (Suffolk)

Legend has it that, when in 870 King Edmund was captured by the Danes at the Battle of Hoxne, he was later killed by arrows and afterwards beheaded. The head was later discovered thanks to the voice of the dead king himself crying, 'Here, Here'. The 'here' was a clearing where sat a wolf guarding the missing part of the royal body. 'The shrine of the king and the cradle of the law', reads the motto. Illustration from the 1894 edition of *The Book of Public Arms*.

BUXTON (Derbyshire)

Well known in Buxton are its eight thermal springs which bring many to the town seeking their healing properties. For the arms granted in 1917, eight circles of blue and silver wavy lines (the heraldic symbol for wells or fountains) together with the Rod of Æsculapius (for health) in gold were placed upon a green shield. 'O all ye springs, bless ye the Lord', translates the motto. Above the shield and forming the crest stands a buck, which not only alludes to the town's name, but is commemorative of the Dukes of Devonshire who played an important role in Buxton's development.

CALNE (Wiltshire)

The silver feathers recall that Calne was once part of the Duchy of Cornwall. Note how each pierces a gold scroll. The tower, with its upper domed story, is also silver and together with the feathers is set upon a black ground. Illustration from the 1894 edition of *The Book of Public Arms*.

CAMBERWELL (London)

For centuries those unable to walk or were disfigured in some way visited the medicinal springs at this South London borough. Camberwell, in fact, means the well of the crooked folk. Granted in 1901, the arms show two wells and the punning motto 'All's Well'. And here too in the crest, we remember St Giles, the patron of cripples who himself was made lame by a wounded hind that he had attempted to help. Careful were the heralds to show the poor creature with drops of blood and, piercing its neck, an arrow. But the latter is absent in the Edwardian postcard, illustrated. The chevron and cinquefoils seen in the top right quarter of the shield are from the arms of Edward Alleyn who in the early part of the seventeenth century held the manor of Dulwich and part of Camberwell. The lion is from neighbouring Peckham, once again its owner enjoying a portion of Camberwell.

CAMBRIDGE (Cambridgeshire)

Looking more like a three-turreted castle, the crest from the arms of Cambridge is in fact on record as representing the bridge at the farthest navigable part of the River Cam from which the university town takes its name. The history of Cambridge will reveal that once the town owed much to its river traffic from the coast. The ships and seahorses recall this. Illustrated is the Cambridge arms as depicted in the 1894 edition of *The Book of Public Arms* and a photograph showing how the Cambridgeshire Regiment adopted the arms as its cap badge. The silver and brass badge also includes a superimposed shield bearing the three open crowns from the arms of the Isle of Ely and scrolls bearing the title of the regiment and the battle honour 'SOUTH AFRICA 1900-01'. The Cambridge arms were granted 7 June 1575.

CAMBRIDGESHIRE

The 1894 edition of *The Book of Public Arms* notes that the county has no armorial bearings, 'but those of the town of Cambridge sometimes appear to be made use of.'

CAMELFORD (Cornwall)

In both editions of *The Book of Public Arms* mention is made that Camelford had no armorial bearings and that Berry gives a silver camel passing through a ford of water, an obvious pun of the town's name. A C Fox-Davies includes the sketch illustrated in his 1915 edition.

CANNOCK (Staffordshire)

A seal is on record which shows a tree, beneath which is a miner's pick and shovel in reference to the town's coal industry. Cannock was a small rural town until mining activity increased during the mid-to-late nineteenth century.

CANTERBURY (Kent)

'Argent three Cornish choughs two and one sable, beaked and legged gules, on a chief of the last a lion passant guardant or.' This the heraldic description on the arms registered by the College of Heralds in 1619, but they were in use long before that. Official documents dated 1380 have been noted. Observing Canterbury's strong ties to royalty, included is the Lion of England. And for Thomas Becket, Archbishop of Canterbury from 1162 until his murder in 1170, we have the three black birds (choughs, common to Cornwall) from his arms. The illustration is from a Ja-Ja postcard of 1905.

CARLISLE (Cumberland)

A C Fox-Davies notes in both editions of *The Book of Public Arms* that Carlisle has no armorial bearings, but illustrates its seal. The shield on the left is thought to have come from Sir William de Carlyell who bore a red cross on a gold ground. The red roses, records C Wilfrid Scott-Giles, are possibly

23

in reference to Sir William's Lancastrian sympathies during the Wars of the Roses. Also illustrated is a Wills's cigarette card of 1905 and the ship's badge of HMS *Carlisle*.

CARSHALTON (Surrey)

Arms were not granted to Carshalton Urban District Council until 1952, but an early seal is on record which displays a Tudor rose.

CASTLE-RISING (Norfolk)

A C Fox-Davies in both editions of *The Book of Public Arms* states that Castle-Rising has no armorial bearings, but 'The seal represents a castle with three towers domed, on each a pennon, in the centre over the gateway a latticed window.' The castle at this small town was erected some time before 1176 by William de Albini, first Earl of Sussex.

CHARD (Somerset)

Both editions of *The Book of Public Arms* state that Chard has no armorial bearings, the first (1894) volume, however, suggesting that the two birds on the oval seal illustrated are thought to be peacocks.

CHATHAM (Kent)

Two ancient ships, each with masts, sails and red colours flying above a red and gold chequered band. Below, and passing through a wreath of laurel, a trident crosses a sword. A naval crown serves as a crest. Inspired by those of Pitt, Earl of Chatham, these were the arms granted on 1 August 1891. The importance of Chatham as a naval base are reflected in its charges, ships and the crown for the Royal Navy, the sword, trident and laurel wreath representing the Royal Marines. Illustration from the 1915 edition of *The Book of Public Arms*.

CHEADLE AND GATLEY (Cheshire)

The parish of Etchells-in-Stockport and the villages of Cheadle Moseley and Cheadle Bulkeley were merged as the Cheadle and Gatley Urban District in 1894 and the arms assumed held references to all three. Here we have the three bulls' heads of the Bulkeley family, the millpicks and eagles of the Moseleys and three empty lozenges representing Etchells-in-Stockport.

CHELMSFORD (Essex)

On a silver ground, crossed croziers separate blue lions above a three-arched bridge. Another crozier serves as part of the crest, this time accompanied by crossed swords and an oak wreath. Granted on 6 February 1889, the arms remember the bridging of the River Chelmer in the twelfth century by one of the Bishops of London who held the Manor of Bishop's Hall. The croziers recall this ecclesiastical association. During the sixteenth century Chelmsford passed into the hands of the Mildmay family, and it is their blue lions that we see at the top of the shield. Illustration from the 1915 edition of *The Book of Public Arms*.

CHELSEA (London)

Divided into four quarters by a cross bearing a crozier we find a red shield charged with a winged bull, a lion rampant, a sword between two boars' heads and, looking out, that of a stag. There on Sydney Street since 1824, and where Charles Dickens married Catherine Hogarth in 1836, is Chelsea's parish church of St Mark whose emblem is a winged bull. The lion is for lord of the manor Lord Cadogan, the boars' heads, sword and stag all having a connection with the Sloane family. An ancestor of Lord Cadogan gained Chelsea by marriage to a Sloane. The crozier is for the Abbot of Westminster who was lord of the manor during the reign of Edward the Confessor. The motto was taken from Psalm 127 i:—'Except the Lord keep the city, the watchman waketh but in vain'. Chelsea's arms were granted in 1903. Illustration from an Edwardian postcard.

CHELTENHAM (Gloucestershire)

On the shield, pigeons, an oak tree and two open books divided by a cross. Another pigeon serves as a crest as it sits on a blue and silver ball representing a fountain, between two branches of oak. The arms shown in this 1905 postcard were granted 26 February 1877. Two open books represent the two important seats of learning in this Gloucestershire town, the Ladies' College and College for Boys. In the cross, we remember Edward the Confessor who once owned much land in the area. Blue is uses as a background to these devices, the colour representing the town's healthy spa waters. The birds recall how it was the sighting of pigeons drinking from a spring that led to the discovery of this popular tourist attraction. An oak tree on the shield, its branches also part of the crest, symbolises Cheltenham's standing as one of the country's leading garden towns. The town's avenues of trees are, too, a main attraction for visitors. Cheltenham's fame indeed lies in its motto, 'Through health and learning.'

CHEPPING WYCOMBE (Buckinghamshire)

On a grassy mound a chained white swan with a ducal coronet around its neck, the swan much associated with the county and the Staffords, Dukes of Buckingham. 'Industry enriches', translates the motto.

CHESHIRE

Three gold garbs on a blue ground form the centre of a Garter belt crowned by an earl's coronet, its supporters being two red dragons, each holding a silver ostrich feather affixed to a scroll. The Garter, coronet, dragons and ostrich feathers are all connected with the Prince of Wales, the Earl of Chester. Illustration from the 1894 edition of *The Book of Public Arms*.

CHESTER (Cheshire)

A gold lion, together with a silver wolf, support a divided red and blue shield: lions on the red, wheatsheaves on the blue. 'Let men of the ancient virtues worship the Ancient of Days', translates the motto. Here we have the Royal Arms of England (three lions) joined with those of the old Earls of Chester (three wheatsheaves). We also have an old heraldic custom of halving shields from top to bottom when two were joined as one. Hence lions with no tails and only half of the Earl's wheatsheaves. The sword serving as a crest is to represent justice, the wolf coming from Hugh Lupus, the first Earl of Chester. C Wilfrid Scott-Giles points out that the lion supporter 'is probably that of Ferrers, Earl of Derby, who married a sister and coheiress of Ranulph, Earl of Chester, the last of the line of Hugh Lupus.' Chester's arms were granted in 1580. Illustration by Paxton Chadwick and from *The Arms of Cheshire* by John N C Lewis.

CHESTERFIELD (Derbyshire)

The 1894 edition of *The Book of Public Arms* illustrates a seal which features a representation of a pomegranate tree. C Wilfrid Scott-Giles notes that this device was in use by Chesterfield during the reign of Elizabeth I and is thought to have been derived from the pomegranate of Granada adopted as a badge by Henry VIII upon his marriage to Katherine of Aragon. But other records state that a pomegranate was in use by Chesterfield long before Tudor times. The fruit was replaced by a blue lozenge during the seventeenth century but made a reappearance as the seal of Chesterfield Corporation in 1893.

CHICHESTER (Sussex)

The shield recorded by the College of Arms and illustrated in the 1894 edition of *The Book of Public Arms* shows a gold lion passant on a red ground on the upper part and a pattern of black drops on silver below. A C Fox-Davies points out, however, that a manuscript in Ulster's Office shows the arms with a tower placed in the upper part of the shield. A second illustration shows the shield superimposed upon a three-towered castle.

CHIPPENHAM (Wiltshire)

On the seal, a tree and two shields. A C Fox-Davies refers to *Burke's General Armoury* for details, viz on a silver ground a tree of three large branches. The shields are given as, on the left, blue with ten silver billets (small oblong shapes) and a silver label of five points, on the right, one of gold displaying three armoured legs. C Wilfrid Scott-Giles, having been informed by the town clerk, records that the shields are respectively those of Gascelyn, Lord of the Manor of Sheldon, and Husee, Lord of the Manor of Rowdon. Illustration from the 1915 edition of *The Book of Public Arms*.

CHIPPING NORTON (Oxfordshire)

A two-towered castle with the letters I R and the date February 1606 forms the town's seal. The letters are for Jacobus Rex and referring to James I from whom the charter of incorporation was granted on the date mentioned. The castle at Chipping Norton dates from just after the Norman Conquest. Illustrations from the 1894 edition of *The Book of Public Arms* and an Edwardian postcard.

26

CHIPPING SODBURY (Gloucestershire)

Three lions passant and the date 1680 which was the year the town obtained borough status from King Charles II. Illustration from the 1894 edition of *The Book of Public Arms*.

CHORLEY (Lancashire)

On a red chevron, three silver shields each charged with a cornflower (or bluebottle). Above this, a gold crown on a red ground. Granted on 3 July 1882, Chorley's arms were based on those of the Chorley family. Chorley Hall, now demolished, was built by the de Choleys in the fourteenth century and was painted by John Bird in 1785.

CHRISTCHURCH (Hampshire)

A C Fox-Davies refers to the figure featured on the town seal as 'a saint seated beneath a canopy.' Other authorities offer 'Christ enthroned'. Illustration from the 1894 edition of *The Book of Public Arms*.

CINQUE PORTS (Kent and Sussex)

A shield divided red and blue from top to bottom and charged with three demi gold lions and three demi gold hulks of ships. A C Fox-Davies was of a mind that the combination of the lions of England with three hulks of ships was in reference to the Royal Navy and its association with the several Cinque Ports coastal towns.

CIRENCESTER (Gloucestershire)

A phoenix emerging from flames. C Wilfrid Scott-Giles suggests that the device may have come from Queen Elizabeth I who adopted the phoenix, so it is said, to symbolize her recovery from smallpox.

CLACKTON-ON-SEA (Essex)

Collectors and historians of heraldry will no doubt be aware of those small china models bearing coats of arms: crested china, made as souvenirs for the visitor wishing to take home a reminder of his holiday. W Gurney Benham, in his 1916 book on Essex borough and county arms, points out how it was not beyond the china manufacturer, upon discovering that a certain town had no arms, to invent one. 'In self-defence', notes Mt Benham, 'Clacton Urban Council in the year 1911 formally adopted a device with at least the merit of being correct heraldically and embodying some local history.' Here then in the upper portion of the shield we see heraldry taken from the D'Arcy family of St Osyth, the one-time holders of the Manor of Great Clacton. The crossed swords represent the See of London, Clacton once part of the lands owned by the Bishops of London. The town's church is dedicated to St James (his shells are here too), as is the shield of Essex and a ship as a symbol of Clacton's maritime importance. 'Light, health and happiness', translates the motto.

CLAYTON-LE-MOORS (Lancashire)

With no arms of its own, Clayton-le-Moors made use of those of the Clayton family: a black cross between four red roundels on a silver shield, together with a leopard's forepaw.

CLAYTON WEST (Yorkshire)

A town seal is on record which displays a bee, possible in reference to industry. There were once eleven coal mines in the area, that at Clayton West being named Park Hill.

CLITHEROE (Lancashire)

A castle on a mound with three domed towers, each with a flag flying. Burke gives the colours as a gold castle on a blue ground. C Wilfrid Scott-Giles identifies the castle as that built by Roger de Poictou and dismantled in 1649. Illustration from the 1894 edition of *The Book of Public Arms*.

COCKERMOUTH (Cumberland)

Both editions of *The Book of Public Arms* state that the town has no armorial bearings. Debrett's *House of Commons,* however, shows an elaborate design featuring a combination of intertwined letters.

COLCHESTER (Essex)

Two staves positioned to form a cross, its arms and foot pierced with nails, and three crowns. Heraldically, the cross depicted in the arms of this Essex town is described as being made up of ragged staves. Be it fact or legend, Old King Cole, according to Geoffrey of Monmouth, was the father of Helena, wife of the Emperor Claudius. Colchester, however, regarded Helena as a local princess and recalled her in its arms. She was on a pilgrimage to Palestine around AD 326 when she found the True Cross and built a church in Jerusalem to enshrine it. The three crowns are from the ancient Kingdom of the East Angles. Some illustrations include nails, as with the image from the 1915 edition of *The Book of Public Arms,* but others do not, as in the Edwardian postcard, illustrated. W Gurney Benham's book on Essex borough arms illustrates a common seal which features a representation of St Helena, the patron saint of Colchester, enthroned under an elaborate canopy. He also referes to 'the most ancient of all known seals of Colchester' which depicts a representation of a raven and explains that during the town's history it came under the government of the Danes who are supposed to use this as an emblem. Certainly the bird appears on the flag of the Port of Colchester.

COLNE (Lancashire)

Here, representing the town's important woollen industry, is a fleece and a representation of a cotton plant. In the centre of the shield we see two Roman coins symbolizing the occupation of Colne (called Colunio then) and a fig leaf. The ancient Chapelry of Calne was described as being in the shape of a fig leaf and as broad as it was long, records C Wilfrid Scott-Giles.
The lion crest is from the heraldry of the De Lacys, once Lords of the Manor.

CONGLETON (Cheshire)

Heraldry likes to play on words. Here, in the Congleton arms we have conger eels and tuns, tuns being large casks for holding wine, ale or beer. 'To thee be the band

28

of comrades dedicated', translates the motto. In the crest, the lion is doing its best to keep its balance and from joining the conger eels in the water. The lion is thought to represent Henry de Lacy, Earl of Lincoln who granted the town a charter in the fourteenth century. The 1894 edition of *The Book of Public Arms* provides two illustrations.

CORBRIDGE (Northumberland)

A cross between four human heads. Both editions of *The Book of Public Arms* offer no illustration, but A C Fox-Davies notes that a representation of the Corbridge shield can be seen as part of the County of Northumberland arms. Another source states that the seal was awarded to Corbridge by King John in the 1200s 'when it was second only to Newcastle in the area.'

CORFE CASTLE (Dorsetshire)

No illustration in either edition of *The Book of Public Arms*, but A C Fox-Davies quotes a description from Berry: 'Hath not any armorial ensign. The seal, which is very ancient, is on a ground dispersed with martlets and fleur-de-lis. A castle with two towers, surmounted with a tower in the centre, over each tower an ostrich feather.' The castle looks over the village and dates from the tenth century. It was the site in 978 of the murder of Edward the Martyr.

CORNWALL

Long the sign of a pawnbroker has been three balls. The best of this honourable trade was thought to be in Cornwall, and it was in King John's time that five pawnbrokers, Ben Levi of Truro, Ben Ezra from Penzance, a Mr Moses who resided in Mevagissey and two others, formed the Ancient and Honourable Association of Pawnbrokers. Cash was needed to finance the war in France, the King putting up his crown to raise the necessary cash. A trade mark was needed by the five, so up came the idea that five times three equals fifteen. Hence the fifteen roundels seen in the county's arms. The five were keen to conduct their business in a proper way and would introduce the rule that no decision could be made without there being a quorum of all five members. With this in mind, along came the motto 'One and all'. The first illustration is taken from the 1915 edition of *The Book of Public Arms* while the second shows a member of the 3rd Cornwall Artillery Volunteer Corps which was formed in 1859 at Fowey.

COVENTRY (Warwickshire)

An elephant as a symbol of strength and wisdom, a castle for its strength and security. Above both sits a cat symbolising watchfulness. The motto translating as 'Court of the Prince' and possibly recalls Edward the Black Prince's connection with the city. Illustrations from the 1915 edition of *The Book of Public Arms*, a Wills's cigarette card of 1905 and as used by the Royal Navy as a badge for HMS *Coventry*.

CRAYFORD (Kent)

Crayford Urban District Council used the white horse and motto *'Invicta'* of Kent.

CREWE (Cheshire)

Important to this Cheshire town since it was established in 1840 was its railway works. Producing locomotives for the London, Midland & Scottish Railway Company, the factory was to play a key role in railway history and in transportation as a whole. With this in mind the arms shown a locomotive and tender as a crest, while the shield illustrates several modes of transport—the canal, stagecoach, horses—of the past. Two illustrations, the first from the 1894 edition of *The Book of Public Arms*, the second in colour from *The Arms of Cheshire* by John N C Lewis, illustrated by Paxton Chadwick, which was published in 1949.

CROMER (Norfolk)

Popular was the town as a seaside resort, an attraction too was the Cromer crab which provided a major source of income to local fisherman. So popular was the place that its road signs boasted 'Gem of the Norfolk Coast'. But not popular at all was its crow insignia; there are three of them on the town's arms. In 1932, according to one newspaper report, the council came under attack from local fishermen who were blaming their low catches on a recently-erected crow weather vain. The crow, it was said, is 'a bird of ill-omen.' Others joined the campaign adding to the fisherman's reasoning that the crow was an emblem of death, disaster and destruction along the east coast during the ninth century. They were referring to the Danes who believed that the appearance of a crow in battle determined its outcome.

CROMPTON (Lancashire)

A seal is on record which shows the arms of Lancashire County Council with, below, a representation of a spinning wheel. Farming is noted as being the main industry of the area, but many supplemented their income by hand-loom woollen weaving. But, come the Industrial Revolution, cotton mills dominated the town.

CROYDON (Surrey)

An interlaced cross divides the shield into four quarters: in the first, three birds; three black crosses for the second; another (blue this time) for the third and for the fourth, a red embattled wall. For the crest, a sword forms a cross with a lance, a ball made up of silver and blue represents a fountain and a bishop's crozier lays horizontal below. Around all, two tufts of rye-grass tied with gold bands. These were the arms granted on 10 August 1886. C Wilfrid Scott-Giles mentions a document issued by Croydon Corporation that states that the birds, three Cornish choughs, are there to represent the County of Surrey. But, remarks the author of *Civic Heraldry in England & Wales,* 'it is difficult to understand why they should have been chosen…' The birds are from the arms of Thomas Becket and can be seen on the arms of Canterbury. Mr Scott-Giles goes on to suggest that the choughs, as is the case regarding the three black crosses, are more likely to recall Croydon's association with the Archbishops of Canterbury. The single cross in the third quarter is that of Archbishop Whitgift who founded the grammar school at Croydon in 1596 and the embattled design is there to suggest a town wall. The heraldic symbol for a fountain is a ball with silver and blue wavy lines and we see it here in the crest representing the springs which come from the chalk hill responsible for the town's name—'croie dune'. Croydon is well known for its production of rye-grass. Illustration from the 1894 edition of *The Book of Public Arms*.

CUMBERLAND

A C Fox-Davies records that the county has no arms of its own but uses a seal based on that of Carlisle, on a shield a plain cross between four roses, a fifth in the centre of the cross. The shield is set upon a rose.

DAGENHAM (Essex)

Arms were not officially granted until 1936, but in use prior to that were the arms of Essex. The three seaxes, however, were reversed.

DARLINGTON (Durham)

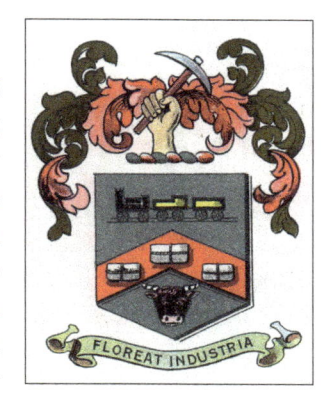

'Locomotion No1'; this was the name of the first locomotive to run on a public railway, hauling passengers for the new Stockton & Darlington Railway on 27 September 1825. See it preserved at the Darlington Railway Centre and Museum; see it also on two illustrations, the first from the 1915 edition of *The Book of Public Arms,* the second from an Edwardian postcard. In the bull's head we have a local celebrity in the form of 'Comet', a shot-horn bull bred by pioneering breeders the Colling brothers of Ketton near Darlington. The bull's head and wool packs are representative of Darlington being a market town. Motto, 'Let us seek the best'.

DARTFORD (Kent)

Until arms were granted to the borough council in 1933, Dartford Urban District Council used those of Kent.

DARTMOUTH (Devonshire)

The kingly figure seen seated in the hull of a ship is thought to be Edward III who had granted a charter to the town. Certainly Dartmouth had been a home of the Royal Navy from his reign and had suffered two surprise attacks during the Hundred Years War. Also seen in the illustrations are a crescent and star, two crusading emblems which possibly allude to the fact that Dartmouth was used as the sailing port for the Crusades of 1147 and 1190. The images are from the 1915 edition of *The Book of Public Arms* and an Edwardian postcard.

DARWEN (Lancashire)

Three sprigs of cotton on a gold ground with, between them, blue wavy lines representing the River Darwen from which the town gets its name. Here too, in the form of a crest, is a miner and a shuttle, these and the cotton representing local industries. Certainly Darwen was an important centre for the textile industry during the Industrial Revolution; Samuel Crompton who invented the spinning mule was once resident in the town. The illustrations are from the 1915 edition of *The Book of Public Arms* and a Wills's cigarette card from 1905.

DAVENTRY (Northamptonshire)

'When the Council required a seal', writes W Edgar in *Borough Hill, Daventry, and its History*, '…the heralds of the period could evidently conceive of no better device than a rebus upon the word as generally spoken.' The author refers to the pronouncing of Daventry as 'Dane tre' and describes the figure holding an axe as 'a savage nondescript, half Highlander, half Saracen, designed to represent a Dane, who stands with his hatchet ready to cut down a devoted and inoffensive tree.' Legend has it that Danish settlers planted an oak tree at the top of Borough Hill which overlooks the town, its purpose to mark the centre of England. Illustration from the 1894 edition of *The Book of Public Arms*.

DEAL (Kent)

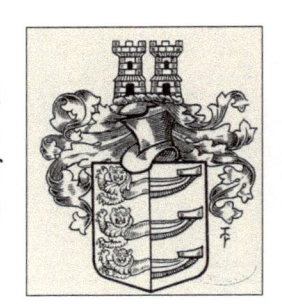

Here we have the familiar half lions and half ships of the Cinque Ports on a shield divided red and blue, with the addition of two towers as a crest. Built by Henry VIII between 539 and 1540, Deal Castle was an artillery fort used for the purpose of defending the Downs anchorage off the coast against invaders. Illustration from the 1915 edition of *The Book of Public Arms*.

DENTON (Lancashire)

The device adopted by Denton Urban District Council was devised to represent the union of the townships of Denton and Haughton, both important in the hat-making industry. The shield is divided and represents two local families, the Dentons (two red bars and three red cinquefoils), and the Haughtons, who had black and silver bars. A beaver crest was included to represent the hat industry. Felt hat manufacture has been recorded in Denton as early as 1702, the year 1825 seeing some twenty-five manufacturers providing regular employment in the two towns.

DEPTFORD (London)

Once Deptford was situated geographically in two counties: Surrey, represented by the three Cornish choughs in the first quarter of the shield, and Kent from whose arms comes the white horse seen in the fourth. The Royal Dockyard at Deptford was founded by Henry VIII and this is symbolized by the representation of a ship on the stocks in the second quarter of the shield while the third shows Peter the Great of Russia seated on a wooden log and holding a shipwright's adze. It was in 1698 that the founder of the Russian Navy, in admiration of English shipbuilding, came to Deptford to learn practical details of the craft whilst lodging at the diarist John Evelyn's house in Sayers Court, Deptford. The tridents in the crest and dolphin supporters confirm Deptford's long association with the sea and ships.

DERBY (Derbyshire)

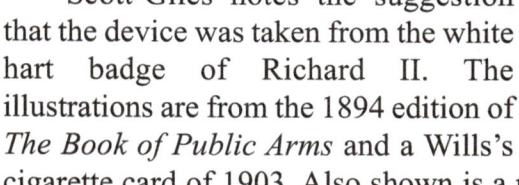

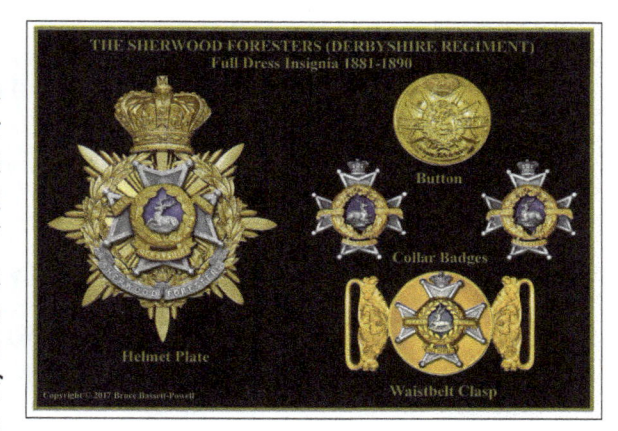

A stag lodged among trees was an ancient seal of the town, but a later version showed on a silver shield the animal on a green mound enclosed within park gates. C W Scott-Giles notes the suggestion that the device was taken from the white hart badge of Richard II. The illustrations are from the 1894 edition of *The Book of Public Arms* and a Wills's cigarette card of 1903. Also shown is a photograph, courtesy of Bruce Bassett-Powell/ Rob Bennett and the Uniformology website, of badges belonging to the Sherwood Foresters (Derbyshire) Regiment.

DERBYSHIRE

Both editions of *The Book of Public Arms* mention that the county had no armorial bearings but acknowledges the use for some time of a crowned rose. Illustration from the 1894 edition.

DEVISES (Wiltshire)

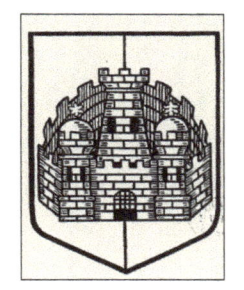

The castle shown on the red and blue divided shield of Devises is that built by Roger, Bishop of Salisbury, during the reign of Henry I and later destroyed by Cromwell during the Civil War. A black star is shown above each of the gateway towers. The first illustration is taken from the 1915 edition of *The Book of Public Arms*, the second showing how the castle was used by the Devises firm of E & W Anstie as a trade mark.

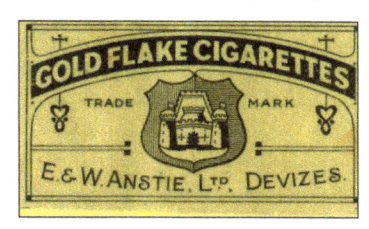

DEVONPORT (Devonshire)

Much of the history of the Royal Navy and the sea lies in Devonport, its arms showing naval crowns, dolphins, an anchor and a ship under construction. Dating from 1690, when a stone dock was built for the Admiralty by the name of Plymouth Dock, the working population grew until, in 1811, it stood at more than 30,000. With permission of King George IV, the town's name was change to Devonport in 1823. The illustrations are from the 1915 edition of *The Book of Public Arms* and a Wills's cigarette card of 1905.

DEVONSHIRE

Both editions of *The Book of Public Arms* mention that the county has no armorial bearings. A seal, however, is illustrated in the 1894 volume which shows three shields: that of the City of Exeter, another of Lord Clinton, Lord Lieutenant of the county and chairman of the council, and that belonging to the Earl of Morley who was vice-chairman.

DEWSBURY (Yorkshire)

A gold cross between two white owls on a black ground. Below this a gold and blue chequered pattern. Another owl standing in front of a blue cross serves as a crest. The motto translates as 'God is our refuge and strength'. These were the arms granted in 1893, the chequered pattern coming from the Earls de Warenne, the owls courtesy of the Savile family and the crosses from the Copleys, three important Dewsbury names. Illustration from the 1915 edition of *The Book of Public Arms*.

DONCASTER (Yorkshire)

On a red ground, a silver castle and gold crown. The crest has a gold lion carrying a blue banner on which the castle appears on lines representing water. Doncaster Castle was built on the site of a Roman fort which stood on the banks of the River Don. Illustration from the 1894 edition of *The Book of Public Arms*.

DORCHESTER (Dorsetshire)

The town, notes both editions of *The Book of Public Arms*, has no armorial bearings, but shown in the 1894 volume is a seal which has a castle upon which is superimposed an early Royal Arms shield of four quarters: one and four, France and England, two Scotland, three, Ireland. Dorchester Castle dates before 1154 when it was in the possession of the Earl of Cornwall; the building is now occupied by Dorchester Prison.

DORSETSHIRE

Both editions of *The Book of Public Arms* note that the county had no armorial bearings but illustrated in the 1894 volume is a county seal of three lions passant.

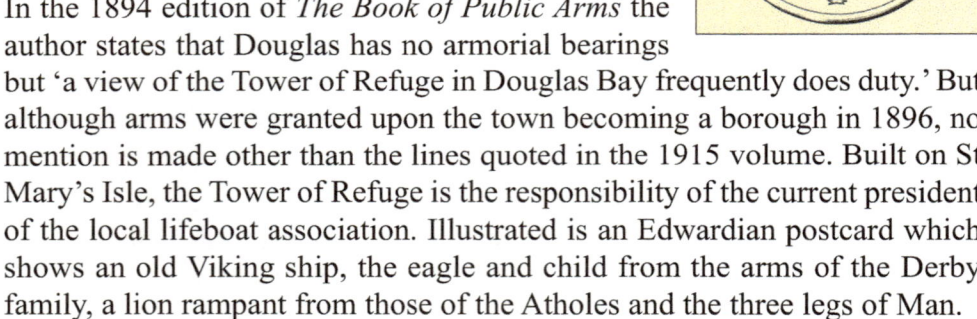

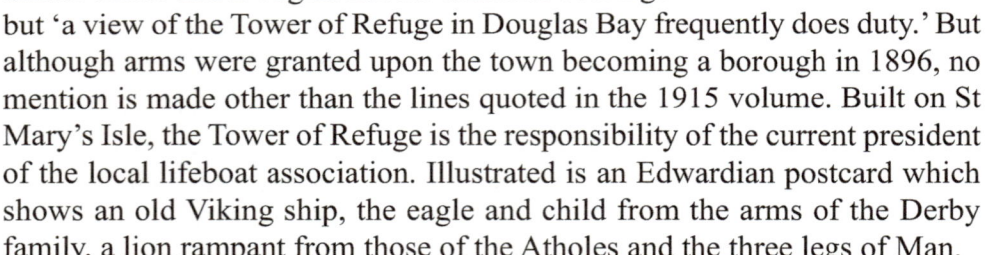

DOUGLAS (Isle of Man)

In the 1894 edition of *The Book of Public Arms* the author states that Douglas has no armorial bearings but 'a view of the Tower of Refuge in Douglas Bay frequently does duty.' But although arms were granted upon the town becoming a borough in 1896, no mention is made other than the lines quoted in the 1915 volume. Built on St Mary's Isle, the Tower of Refuge is the responsibility of the current president of the local lifeboat association. Illustrated is an Edwardian postcard which shows an old Viking ship, the eagle and child from the arms of the Derby family, a lion rampant from those of the Atholes and the three legs of Man.

DOVER (Kent)

A C Fox-Davies illustrates in his 1894 edition of *The Book of Public Arms* the device quoted in Burke's *General Armoury* of a silver cross and four gold leopards' heads on a black ground. In the 1915 edition, however, we see illustrated on a shield the figure of St Martin in the act of dividing his cloak. Here too is the beggar and a border of lions. The shield is given as silver, the lions silver on a red ground. This device is registered at the Heralds' College as being based on a fourteenth-century seal. Not illustrated but mentioned in

34

the 1915 volume are notes referring to the 1574 Visitation of Kent in which a reference is made to 'the common Seal of the Towne and Port of Dover'. Described is the front of the seal, which shows St Martin and the beggar leaving a city gate surrounded by a border of lions, while the reverse has a representation of a ship at sea and the half-lions and half-ships' hulks which we associate with the Cinque Ports. A third illustration is from an Edwardian postcard posted at Dover in 1906. The patron saint of Dover, the Church of St Martin-le-Grand, once stood on the west side of what is now the Market Square.

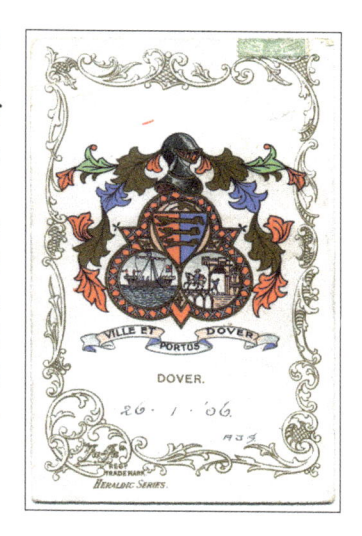

DROITWICH (Worcestershire)

Divided up into five sections, the shield has a sword on a red background placed behind two gold lions. On the other side there are two sections of silver and black squares and another two each with a pair of what is thought to be Indian clubs on a red ground. They are, in fact, wicker mounds used for the manufacture of salt, Droitwich holding a monopoly on this trade for many centuries. The chequered designs represent the table for which the salt was destined. The lions and sword on the left side of the shield are for landowners King John and his brother William of the Long Sword. Illustration from the 1915 edition of *The Book of Public Arms*.

DROYLSDEN (Lancashire)

A shield charged with three diagonal bars (bendlets) was used by the Droylsden Urban District Council. These were from the arms of the Byron family who were Lords of the Manor.

DUDLEY (Worcestershire)

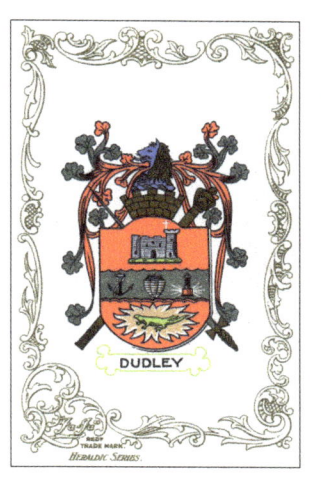

The town's arms, as seen in the 1905 postcard illustrated, offer much evidence as to the area's industrial activity: coal in the miners' lamp, iron from the anchor, while the lizard-like amphibian (a salamander) surrounded by flames refers to the many furnaces of the Black Country. Literature and legend associate salamanders with fire, the creature supposedly being unharmed by flames. Plentiful too are the 'Dudley Bugs' (there's one in the centre of the shield), fossilized trilobites found in the limestone (another Dudley industry) throughout the West Midlands. Here, too, is Dudley Castle which was built in 1537 by John Dudley.

DUKINFIELD (Cheshire)

The town arms and crest, granted in March 1900, are based on those of the Dukinfield family, the unusual pointed cross also appearing in the arms of Stalybridge. Top left is a raven, the bird known locally as a 'docken' is a rebus and forms part of the town's name origins and the wheatsheaf is taken from the arms of the Prince of Wales, Earl of Chester. Also rarely seen is the type of crown used in the crest. Known as a vallary crown, with its palisades set on a rim, it has issuing from it a forearm, the hand of which is clasping a blue shield charged with the sun, and two ostrich feathers. Illustration by Paxton Chadwick and from *The Arms of Cheshire* by John N C Lewis.

DUNSTABLE (Bedfordshire)

A C Fox-Davies in both editions of his *The Book of Public Arms* referes to the device featured in his 1915 illustration as an ale warmer. But C Wilfrid Scott-Giles, although agreeing that these are the actual arms in use, states that they are, in reality, a corruption of those used by Dunstable Priory. Burke recalls these and describes them as having a horseshoe interlaced to a staple and affixed to the lower part of a pile, a wedge-shaped figure descending from the top of the shield. The Priory arms were used by Dunstable as its seal, but it is suggested (C W Scott-Giles again) that lack of skill by engravers over the centuries has corrupted the pile by offering it as an ale-warmer.

DUNWICH (Suffolk)

A C Fox-Davies mentions Dunwich in both editions of *The Book of Public Arms* but offers no illustrations. There is the following description of the town's seal, however: 'a ship of three masts upon the waves, the mainmast ensigned with a flag of St George, the sails furled, the other two masts broken off at the round top, on the water four fish swimming to the dexter.' Dunwich's port and shipbuilding industry were prosperous until several storm surges during the thirteenth and fourteenth centuries destroyed many buildings and carried away much land.

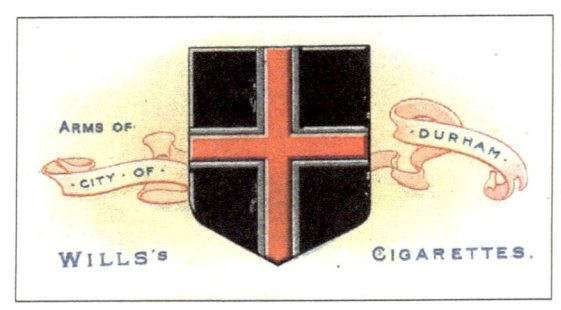

DURHAM (City)

Based on the arms of the See of Durham, a simple black shield with, placed upon it, a white cross and on that another of red. Illustration from a Wills's cigarette card.

DURHAM (County)

The county used the shield of the See of Durham, a gold cross and four gold lions on a blue ground.

EALING (Middlesex)

In the 1905 postcard illustrated we see the arms granted on 22 February three years earlier. Here is an oak tree which is to symbolise that Ealing was growing and flourishing. The three seaxes represent the ancient kingdom of Middle Saxons (Middlesex), while the crossed swords are those of St Paul and the arms of the See of London of which Ealing was once part.

EAST ANGLIA

Mentioned in the 1915 edition of *The Book of Public Arms* only, A C Fox-Davies notes that 'There is no body corporate competent to bear arms or to whom arms could be granted or assigned, but a flag has been invented for use in the Eastern Counties.' He goes on to note and illustrate a device of a red cross on a silver ground upon which is placed a blue shield bearing three gold crowns.

EAST GRINSTEAD (Sussex)

Mentioned, but not illustrated, in both editions of *The Book of Public Arms*, A C Fox-Davies describes the town's seal as a double rose crowned with the words 'Sus' on the left side, and 'Sex' on the right. C Wilfrid Scott-Giles, however, gives a version that has five ostrich feathers within a scroll and between the letters 'DL' (Duchy of Lancaster). He also notes that the device was granted by the Heralds and appeared on the seal presented to the corporation in 1572 by Thomas Cure, the Member of Parliament for the borough.

EAST HAM (Essex)

W Gurney Benham points out in his *Borough & County Arms of Essex* how East Ham was constituted a borough by a charter dated 27 August 1904. It had no grant of arms but uses the device illustrated. In the ship we see reference to the several docks within the area, the crosier to the onetime holder of the manor, Stratford Abbey. The flaming torches indicate progress and learning. W Gurney Bingham referes to the use of the fiery sun, not a crest in the eyes of heraldry, as an indication of the borough spreading glory and greatness.

EAST LOOE (Cornwall)

Mentioned, but not illustrated, in both editions of *The Book of Public Arms*, A C Fox-Davies however provides the following description of the seal which represents 'an antique one-masted vessel, in it a man and a boy, against the side of the hulk three escutcheons each charged with three bends.' Separated by the river, both East and West Looe were prosperous fishing ports.

EAST RETFORD (Nottinghamshire)

A C Fox-Davies illustrates the town's seal in his 1894 edition of *The Book of Public Arms*. It shows two eagles facing each other. He also refers to and quotes from Burke who recorded that 'A rose with a lion of England upon the chief is engraved as the Arms of this town upon some of the oldest plate belonging to the Corporation.' Certainly these arms appeared on a mace presented by Sir Edward Nevile in 1679. Interestingly, when arms were granted to East Retford in November 1940, two birds featured as the only charges on the shield. They were, however, referred to as choughs.

EASTBOURNE (Sussex)

The shield is divided by silver and red horizontal bands and displays a gold rose between two silver stags' heads. There is a representation of a sea-horse as a crest, and the motto '*Meliora sequimur'* (We follow the better things). A C Fox-Davies describes this as the corporation seal and refers to it as 'a bogus Coat-of-Arms'. These very same arms were, in fact, officially granted in 1928. The silver and red bands are from the Badlesmere family, who once held the manor, the stags' heads are those of Cavendish, Duke of Devonshire and the rose, that belonging to the Gilberts. The illustrations are from the 1915 edition of *The Book of Public Arms* and a postcard posted in 1905.

ECCLES (Lancashire)

Too late for inclusion in his 1894 edition of *The Book of Public Arms*, A C Fox-Davies states that Eccles has 'no Armorial Bearings'. A description and illustration was, however, included in 1915, the town's arms having been granted on 7 November 1893. Eccles grew up around its parish church of St Mary's and, it is thought, the ecclesiastical building seen in the lower section of the shield represents this. Another notion is that the Anglo Saxon word describing a place with a recognisable church was 'Ecles'. In the upper section of the shield we see a representation of the steam hammer invented in 1839 by James Nasmyth. Scottish born, he had moved to the Patricroft area of Eccles where he opened the Bridgewater Foundry in August 1836. Also providing much employment to the people of Eccles were the cotton mills, two sprigs of the plant being seen accompanying the steam hammer. The ship and lighthouse crest represent the sea trade which reached the town originally via the River Irwell and later the Manchester Ship Canal. 'All things flourish by labour', reads the motto.

EGHAM (Surrey)

A seal belonging to Egham Urban District Council recalls Runnymede by a parchment with an ancient crown above and the inscription 'Magna Charta, 15 June 1215'. Egham is a town in the Runnymede borough of Surrey.

ELY (Cambridgeshire)

In both editions of *The Book of Public Arms* A C Fox-Davies notes that Ely had no armorial bearings and refers to Berry who records that 'This city is not a corporation, and therefore hath not any Arms.' He goes on to say that those of the Deanery, three gold ducal coronets on a red ground, are used. In the Edwardian postcard of Ely Cathedral and Palace illustrated we see both the arms of the See and Priory.

EPSOM (Surrey)

A seal bearing a castle is on record.

ERITH (Kent)

Not granted until 27 February 1906, the arms of Erith Urban District Council escaped inclusion in the 1894 edition of *The Book of Public Arms*.

In 1915, however, we see a black fleur-de-lis and the red pike fish from the De Luci family (ancient lords of the manor) and, tucked away in the top left-hand-corner, the White Horse of Kent. A running stag in front of a wheatsheaf forms the crest, the latter being from the arms of Wheatley, lords of the manor until 1875. Also associated with the area was Lord Eadley of Belvedere Mansion whose arms included a stag.

ESHER AND THE DITTONS (Surrey)

The urban district council, having no arms of its own, used those of Cardinal Wolsey: a silver cross charged with a red lion and four blue leopards' faces and a red rose between two black Cornish choughs. Thomas Wolsey for a number of years after his fall from favour lived under house arrest at Esher Place.

ESSEX

Three seaxes with gold pommels and silver blades on a red ground. Although not officially granted until 1932, these arms represent the old Kingdom of the East Saxons and were in use for many years before. The second illustration (a blazer badge) shows how the arms featured in the cap badges of the Essex Yeomanry.

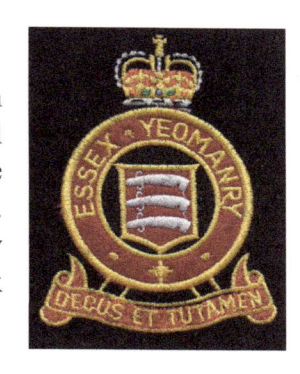

ETON (Buckinghamshire)

Eton Urban District Council used the arms of Eton College which include three silver lilies in reference to the Virgin Mary to whom the college is dedicated.

EVESHAM (Worcestershire)

Grateful to Henry Prince of Wales who gave Evesham its charter of incorporation as a borough in 1604, the several devices on the town's shield granted in 1634 are from his arms. The illustrations are from the 1894 edition of *The Book of Public Arms* and an Edwardian postcard which also shows the arms of Evesham Abbey.

EXETER (Devon)

On a red and black ground, a gold castle representing that known as Rougemont Castle and built into the northern corner of the old Roman city walls. Above, and serving as a crest, is the lion of Richard, Earl of Cornwall who was elected as King of the Romans. It would be Henry III that generously presented Richard with both the city of Exeter and its castle. 'Ever faithful' reads the motto, another royal gift, this time by Elizabeth I. Illustrations: an Edwardian postcard by Faulkner and a detailed photograph provided by the Bruce Bassett-Powell/ Bob Bennett/ Uniformology.com website showing how the Exeter castle was used in the badges of the Devonshire Regiment.

39

EYE (Suffolk)

A C Fox-Davies offers two illustrations in his 1894 edition of *The Book of Public Arms*. The first shows the town's seal which features the word Eye surmounted by a ducal crown together with the legend 'Sigillum Comune Burgi de Eye'. In the second the author illustrates the arms granted in 1592. Here, rising from an Imperial crown, is the golden Star of Innocence and the all-seeing eye of Jehovah. Below, the shield which has white roses and a silver crowned eagle, thought to be derived from the emblems of Queen Elizabeth I, a gold cross and four gold martlets. Both the cross and martlets are from the arms of King Edward the Confessor.

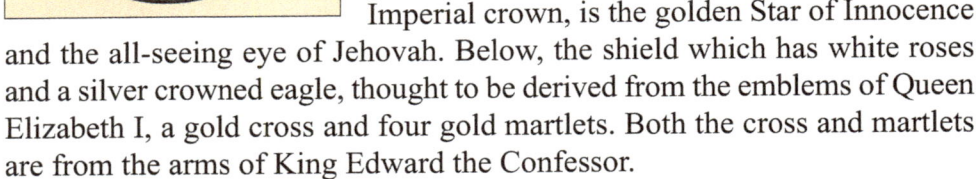

FALMOUTH (Cornwall)

The seal has a double-headed eagle, its wings and breast each charged with a tower. The eagle is from the arms of the Killigrew family, the towers representing Pendennis Castle, built by Henry VIII, and St Mawes Castle, both built to defend the harbour.

FARNHAM (Surrey)

The urban district council used a castle device, a representation of the twelfth-century stronghold built by Henri de Blois, Bishop of Winchester.

FARNWORTH (Lancashire)

A seal has been noted which shows a red lion rampant on a silver ground, this from the family arms of Hulton, of Hulton and Farnworth. The crest is a silver hart's head between two branches of hawthorn. There is a motto, 'Be just and fear not'.

FAVERSHAM (Kent)

Clearly based on the three lions of England, the seals illustrated are from the 1894 edition of *The Book of Public Arms*, and Gale Pedrick's *Borough Seals*. The design also served as arms, the shield being red, the lions half gold, half silver.

FELIXSTOWE (Suffolk)

The urban district council, records C Wilfrid Scott-Giles, made use of a shield divided into three sections, the first charged with a red cross on a gold ground from the heraldry of Roger Bigod, Earl of Norfolk. The second section shows the red saltire cross charged with a gold scallop shell of the See of Rochester, the third a bishop's mitre on six silver and blue lines. So far unexplained are the arms depicted on the Edwardian postcard illustrated which depicts a Danish ship approaching land. On the ship is the figure of a man carrying a cross.

FELLING (Durham)

The crest from the arms of the Brandling family, the stump of a tree in flames, is on record as being used by Felling Urban District Council.

FENTON (Staffordshire)

A C Fox-Davies points out that Fenton has no armorial bearings and, 'moreover, not yet having risen above the dignity of a local board, is not entitled to bear them.' However, he does describe and illustrate those that have 'very extensive use'. As can be seen from the illustration, the shield is divided into quarters, one showing a vase or soup tureen, another two pottery kilns, a third a pit head and a fourth a garb and plough. The four, of course, represent local industries. The goat's head crest is thought to be from the Baker arms, a local potteries family for many years. By the 1850s firms such as Coalport and Bakers were giving employment to many in the town.

FINSBURY (London)

Richard Crosley, in his book on London coats of arms, notes that the borough had no official grant of arms, but in 1900 the council adopted a design for its common seal 'which is representative of the six parishes now included in the area.' The design consists of six shields within a shield, the parishes represented being: Old Cripplegate, Charterhouse, Clerkenwell, St Luke's, St Botolph's and St Sepulchre's.

FLEETWOOD (Lancashire)

The Fleetwood Urban District Council seal bears a shield upon which is a ship and lighthouse. Also shown are the arms of Sir Peter Hesketh Fleetwood and a railway locomotive. Sir Peter was the principal landowner of the area and as High Sheriff and Member of Parliament had the idea to develop the town as a busy seaport and railway centre. The distinguished Victorian architect Decimus Burton was employed to design a number of civic buildings and was responsible for the building of two lighthouses.

FOLKESTONE (Kent)

A C Fox-Davies offers no illustration in either edition of *The Book of Public Arms* but refers to a seal showing an ancient ship upon waves, 'towered at each end, a man's head appearing above the battlements of each, and at the masthead a turret, and a man in the body of the boat, and another in the stern turret.' Originally just a small fishing village, Folkestone's future as an important seaport began in 1807 when an Act of Parliament was passed to build a pier and harbour, the work to be carried out by Thomas Telford.

FOWEY (Cornwall)

Mentioned, but not illustrated in both editions of *The Book of Public Arms*, A C Fox-Davies however referes to Berry's *Dictionary of Heraldry*: 'The seal seems to be originally intended for an armorial ensign, viz., on a shield a ship of three masts on the sea, her topsail furled. The legend around it, "Sigillum oppida de Fowy, Anno Dom, 1702"'. Illustration from an old map.

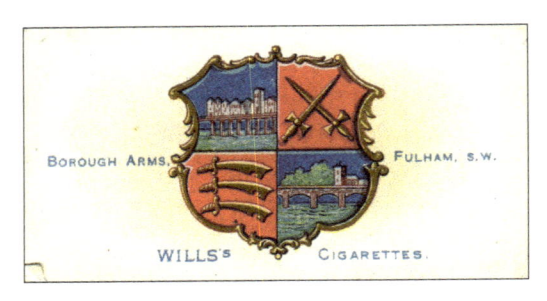

FULHAM (London)

It would not be until 1927 that official arms were granted to this London borough. In use prior to that, however, was the shield shown on the Wills cigarette card of 1905, illustrated. For centuries Fulham was the rural seat of the Bishops of London, the crossed swords of St Paul represent the Bishopric. The three in the third quarter are for Middlesex. Putney and Fulham are linked across the Thames by Putney Bridge and we see on the shield representations of both the former structure (first quarter), opened in 1729, and its 1886 replacement (fourth quarter). Medieval Churches stand at either end of the bridge, St Mary's on the Putney side, All Saints in Fulham. Putney Bridge has been the starting place for the annual Oxford and Cambridge Boat Race since 1845.

GATESHEAD (Durham)

A double play on words, possibly, for this Tyne and Wear town. *Bede's Ecclesiastical History of the English People* refers to the place as 'ad caput capreae'—at the goat's head. Goat became Gate, the latter device of a castle gateway appearing in the town's arms for no other reason than its allusion to the first syllable. 'The head is set amongst the clouds', reads the motto. The arms illustrated are from the 1894 edition of *The Book of Public Arms* and were used unofficially by Gateshead Corporation until 1932 when a similar device including two crosses representing the Palatine of Durham was granted.

GILLINGHAM (Kent)

On the arms granted in 1904, the red cross of St George divides the shield into four quarters, this together with the charges within reflecting the wording of the motto, 'With fort and fleet for home and England'. The origins of the harp are unknown, but the sprig of bloom in the fourth quarter is in reference to close-by Bromley. Moving to the crest we are reminded of Gillingham's naval connections and a battle between Edmund Ironside and Canute which took place in 1016 at, according to the Anglo-Saxon Chronicle, Peonnan near Gillingham.

GLASTONBURY (Somerset)

A C Fox-Davies notes that Glastonbury had no armorial bearings, but shows the device used on the corporation's notepaper: a mitre in front of two crossed croziers with the motto '*Floret Ecclesia Anglicana*'. Both editions of *The Book of Public Arms* do not record colours, but C W Scott-Giles gives gold on blue, as shown on the Edwardian postcard illustrated.

GLOSSOP (Derbyshire)

With no armorial bearings for the town, both editions of *The Book of Public Arms* refer to the corporation seal: a lion above a cap of estate (sometimes called a cap of maintenance) together with the motto '*Virtus Veritas Libertas*' (Virtue, Truth and Freedom). This is the crest from the arms of Lord Howard of Glossop. The date 1866 referes to the year Glossop was created a municipal borough. Illustration from the 1894 edition.

GLOUCESTER (Gloucestershire)

The shield of the arms confirmed in 1652 shows three red chevrons and ten roundels on a gold ground. The crest is made up of a red lion holding a broadsword in one hand and a trowel in the other. Red lions holding swords also provide the supporters, the motto *'Fides Invicta triumphat'*, translating as 'Unconquered faith triumphs'. The chevrons are from the arms of the Clares, Earls of Gloucester and the roundels those of the See of Worcester. The swords represent those carried before the mayor on ceremonial occasions, a tradition authorised via a charter granted by Richard III in 1483. The trowel refers to industry. The second of the two illustrations shows how the arms were used in the badges of the Gloucestershire Regiment.

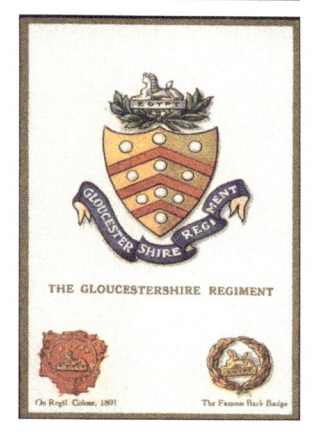

The above arms are described as the 'Commonwealth' arms, but also in use by the city is a device known as the 'Tudor' arms. I'm grateful to the 'Heraldry of the World' website for the accompanying illustration and description. Richard Duke of Gloucester, later King Richard III, granted Gloucester its charter of incorporation in 1483 and it is the boar's head from his heraldry that appears at the top of the shield. The roses are apparently representing the Houses of Lancaster and York. In the lower part of the shield horseshoes and nails represent the city's ancient trades and the sword piercing a cap of maintenance.

GLOUCESTERSHIRE

The county seal bears a cinquefoil in the centre of which is depicted a fleece between two teazles. This to represent the famous Cotswold sheep and the cloth manufacturers around the Stroud Valley. There was once much mining activity in the Forest of Dean and this is symbolized in the seal by two miners' picks. The ancient forest itself is represented by five acorns placed in the cinquefoil. Agriculture also provides employment, for which we see a wheatsheaf.

GODALMING (Surrey)

Important to the town for centuries was its wool production, a fact recalled in the lower section of the shield by a silver woolpack on a red and black ground. Above, and on silver this time, is charged a rose indicating how Godalming received its first Borough Charter during the seventeenth year of Elizabeth's reign. Here too are shields in recollection of Sir George More (left), the first lord of the manor, and John Perrier (right) who was the borough's first warden.

GODMANCHESTER (Huntingdonshire)

The 1894 edition of *The Book of Public Arms* notes that Godmanchester had no armorial bearings, but mentions a seal consisting of a fleur-de-lis with trefoils between the petals. There are also the words *'Commune Sigillum G'mecestre'*. Godmanchester had been a royal manor for a number of years prior to its first charter from King John in 1212.

GOOLE (Yorkshire)

A seal is on record that shows a ship under steam and sail. Above it, the word 'Advance'. Certainly the town did much towards the advance of coal transportation by sea, Thomas Hamond Bartholomew's floating dock, capable of handling large sea-going ships, being constructed during the 1820s. In the detail from an Edwardian postcard illustrated, a rose has been added.

GOSPORT (Hampshire)

C Wilfrid Scott-Giles in his 1933 edition of *Civic Heraldry of England & Wales* mentions that the town has no arms; the corporation, however, uses the device of the Norman ship in which Henry of Blois landed at Gosport. One of five sons of Stephen II, Count of Blois, Henry was brought to England by King Henry I to be Abbot of Glastonbury and on 4 October 1129 was given the bishopric of Winchester. There is, however, an Edwardian postcard which illustrates the seal of Gosport and most likely a representation of Henry of Blois.

GRAMPOUND (Cornwall)

Both editions of *The Book of Public Arms* note that Grampound had no armorial bearings but describe the town seal as representing a bridge of two arches over a river, the right end of which has a tree issuing from the base against the bridge. In the centre of the bridge is a shield 'of the arms of the family Cornwall [Richard, Earl of Cornwall], namely, argent, a lion rampant gules within a bordure sable.' The name Grampound derives from the Norman French *grand pont* (great bridge) and referes to the town's bridge over the River Fai.

GRANTHAM (Lincolnshire)

A gold and blue chequered pattern forms the centre of the town's shield. Around this is a black border charged with eight silver trefoils. The chequers are from the arms of the Warennes, a local family. The trefoils were possibly included by the town to differentiate their device from that of the Warennes. Illustration from an Edwardian postcard.

GRAVESEND (Kent)

Here on a silver ground is a red tower charged with a gold bull's head breathing flames. He sits in a coronet and was first seen on an old town seal. Around the edge of the shield is a blue border of gold fleurs-de-lis alternating with gold buckles, this granted in 1635 in memory of the Duke of Lennox's association with the town. 'An honour and a protection', reads the motto. Illustrations from the 1915 edition of *The Book of Public Arms* and a 1905 cigarette card.

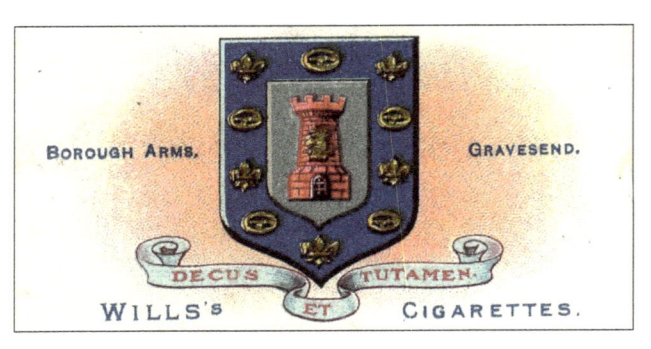

GRAYS THURROCK (Essex)

The urban district council had a device consisting of a shield bearing a tree and a scroll inscribed 'Thor's Oak' together with the three seaxes of Essex. The name derives from Henry de Grai, who was granted the manor in 1195 by Richard I and the Saxon word thurrock meaning the bottom of a ship.

GREAT BEDWIN (Wiltshire)

A domed blue tower with a gold griffin crest above. Illustration from the 1894 edition of *The Book of Public Arms*.

GREAT GRIMSBY (Lincolnshire)

Three black boars' heads and a black chevron on a silver ground. C W Scott-Giles notes that the boars' heads are said to recall the ancient right of the mayor and corporation to hunt the animal in Bradley Woods. He also records that the chevron may be from the arms of a family named Grimsby. Illustration from the 1915 edition of *The Book of Public Arms*.

GREAT TORRINGTON (Devonshire)

The blue-and-white wavy lines represent the River Torridge, the design being based on a fifteenth-century seal.

GREAT YARMOUTH (Norfolk)

An early source tells how, in reference to Great Yarmouth being an important fishing port, three herrings appeared on the town seal. Later, three gold half-lions were added which were joined to the tail ends of the fish. Another source records that it was King Edward III who granted use of the lions from the Royal Arms, in recognition of the patriotic response of Great Yarmouth during the Hundred Years' War. In the illustration we see how the heraldic rule, where metals must not be placed one on the other, is being faithfully observed, the gold lions on red, silver fish on blue.

GREENWICH (London)

The Royal Observatory was built at Greenwich in 1675 as an aid to the advancement of navigation and nautical astronomy. And who would not be aware of the importance of Greenwich to time. With this in mind we see on the shield of the arms granted in 1903 stars and an hour-glass. In the crest we recall the Royal Navy that once used the old Greenwich Palace as a hospital for seamen and later as the Royal Naval College. Illustration from the 1915 edition of *The Book of Public Arms*.

GUILDFORD (Surrey)

Long now in ruins and standing in a public park is the Norman castle represented on the shield of the town's arms. Here too are woolpacks remembering Guildford's once staple trade, a lion, roses, a key hanging in the doorway and a shield from the Royal Arms. A C Fox-

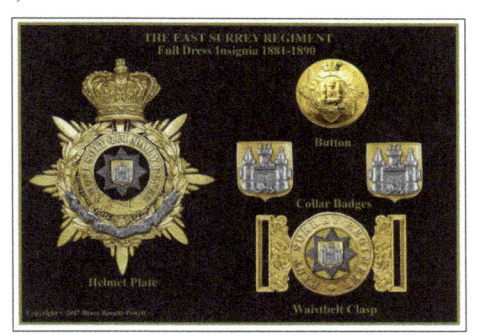

Davies provides illustrations of two versions of the arms in the 1894 edition of *The Book of Public Arms*, the second omitting the roses, shield and key and placing the castle upon on a grassy mound with wavy lines suggesting water. Guildford stands on the rivers Wey and Arun and the Wey Canal. A third image shows how the East Surrey Regiment made use of the arms in its badges, the photo courtesy of Bruce Bassett Powell/Bob Bennett/Uniformology.com).

HACKNEY (London)

Not mentioned at all in the 1894 edition of *The Book of Pubic Arms*, but that for 1915 notes the London borough as having no arms but uses a seal showing a church tower in landscape. The tower in question was that of St Augustine's, all that is left from the thirteenth-century church. The illustration shows how the tower was used by the 10th London Regiment (formed in 1912) as part of its cap badge.

HADLEIGH (Suffolk)

The arms of Hadleigh were granted on 18 February 1618 and feature three silver woolsacks, the town at that time being well known for its manufacture of woollen cloth. Illustration from the 1915 edition of *The Book of Pubic Arms*.

HALE (Cheshire)

A tithe barn was established by the middle of the fifteenth century in Hale Barnes and a representation of this can be seen in the seal adopted in 1900. Also seen is a wheatsheaf and a shield bearing the arms of the Earl of Stamford, Lord of the Manor.

HALIFAX (Yorkshire)

A man's head, dripping with blood and with a halo, appears on a chequered ground of blue and gold. Above his head the word Hales, and below Fax. The chequers are from the arms of John, Earl of Warenne who held the manor of Halifax during the thirteenth century. The man, John the Baptist to whom the parish church is dedicated. He is also remembered by the Holy Lamb crest as it was he who referred to Jesus as the Lamb of God. Halifax once owing much to its wool trade chose John the Baptist for this reason. Illustration from the 1915 edition of *The Book of Pubic Arms*.

HALSTEAD (Essex)

Both editions of *The Book of Public Arms* note that Halstead had no armorial bearings but refers to Burke's *General Armory* which gives a gold coronet on a blue ground. Mr W Gurney Benham writing in his 1916 book *Borough & County Arms of Essex* noted that 'The Halstead Urban District Council, upon its formation thirty years ago, adopted these arms and placed them in the council seal.'

HAMMERSMITH (London)

As a pun on its name, this London borough's crest features crossed hammers, while the charges on the shield are all from the arms of local benefactors. The three horseshoes are those of Sir Nicholas Crisp (1598-1665) who had devised in Hammersmith a new method of making bricks, some of which he donated with a sum of money towards the building of the parish church. Edward Latymer, who

46

died in 1626, did much for the area in the form of providing land for new schools. The two crosses are from his arms. From those of George Pring (died 1824) come the escallop shell. A local surgeon, he did much towards the building of Hammersmith's first bridge across the Thames. Hammersmith's arms were granted on 23 December 1897. Illustration from an Edwardian postcard.

HAMPSHIRE

In both editions of *The Book of Pubic Arms* A C Fox-Davies notes that 'Hampshire, otherwise the county of Southampton, has no armorial bearings. Those of the town of Southampton are frequently quoted and used: often with the colours reversed.' (See Southampton).

HAMPSTEAD (London)

A shield was designed for the Hampstead Vestry in 1897 and it was this that was adopted by the council three years later. The red mitre in the centre of the cross is taken from the arms of the Abbey of Westminster, to which the Manor of Hampstead was granted by King Ethelred in 986. Viscount Campden, one of the Hickes family, purchased the manor after the dissolution of the monasteries in 1539 and it is from his heraldry that were taken the fleur-de-lis and buck's head. The viscount died in 1629 and the manor then passed to the Noels whose arms are represented by the red and gold lattice work at the top of the shield. The silver cross is that of Sir William Langhorne. 'Not for oneself but for all', translates the motto.

HAMPTON WICK (Middlesex)

A device used by the urban district council consists of a stag on a grassy bank gazing down into a stream. Above this a crown.

HANLEY (Staffordshire)

Much is in evidence in the arms of Hanley to its pottery industry, viz three blue jugs and smoking furnaces. In the bottom portion of the shield we see on a red ground the four silver stars from the Wedgwood family. The crest is that of the Ridgway family, John Ridgeway being the first mayor of the newly created borough: a kneeling camel charged with a silver shield bearing the cross of St George. Illustration from an Edwardian postcard.

HARROGATE (Yorkshire)

Well known for its health-giving waters, Harrogate places on its arms the heraldic symbol for a fountain, a roundel with silver and blue wavy lines. Here too, and representing the springs' healing qualities, are two serpents. Credited as the first to discover Harrogate's springs (the sixteenth-century Tewitt Well) was a member of the Slingsby family, the two bugle-horns being from their arms. 'A stronghold famed for its springs', translates the motto.

HARROW (Middlesex)

A silver lion on a blue ground, above the shield two arrows placed within a wreath of laurel. There is a motto, '*Stet fortuna domus*'. In his research A C Fox-Davies, who states that Harrow had no armorial bearings, requested from the vestry clerk a copy of the seal. He replied that the town had no seal and commonly used was the device (a lion rampant) of Harrow School. The illustration used in the 1894 edition of *The Book of Pubic Arms* is shown, together with a photograph of a member of the 27th Middlesex Rifle Volunteer Corps showing how the crossed arrows and wreath were used as badges (image from *Tracing the Rifle Volunteers* by Ray Westlake).

HARTLEPOOL (Durham)

The 1894 edition of *The Book of Pubic Arms*, in which A C Fox-Davies notes that the town has no armorial bearings, but he illustrates a seal of very crude workmanship (his words) showing a hart standing in a pool of water and with a dog springing onto its back.

HARWICH (Essex)

A portcullis and an antique ship. The illustration is from W Gurney Benham's *Borough & County Arms of Essex,* the author explaining in his 1916 book that the portcullis is an especially appropriate emblem for Harwich and signifies its importance as a principal gate and port to England. He also points out that the town was 'a watch-tower or place of defence against unwelcome visitors.' This possibly explains the inclusion of a tower high on the top of the ship's mast.

HASLINGTON (Lancashire)

Here in the cogwheel, pickaxe, spade and shuttle are symbols of the town's industries. People associated with Haslington are also remembered, the lion from the De Lacy Earls of Lincoln who once owned much land in the area, the moorcock in the crest and the six eagles are associated with the Holden family. The red rose between the birds is for Lancaster. A pun here on the town's name as the moorcock holds in its beak a sprig of hazel.

HASTINGS (Sussex)

A shield divided red and blue bearing in its centre a gold lion. Above and below are demi-lions joined to the stern ends of silver ships. Very similar to the arms of the Cinque Ports, with its three half-lions and ships, C W Scott-Gilles pointing out that the inclusion of the whole lion is said to indicate the status of Hastings as the chief port of the group. Illustrations are from the 1894 edition of *The Book of Pubic Arms* and an old blazer badge.

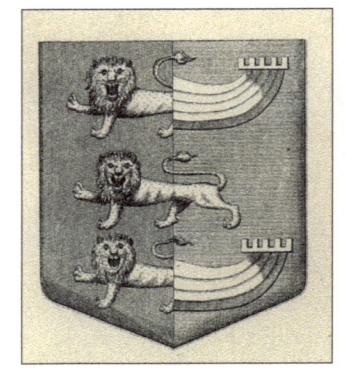

48

HAZEL GROVE AND BRAMHALL (Cheshire)

A shield divided into four sections by a red cross. In the first quarter a gold lion on a black ground, the second a sprig of hazel with three red nuts, the third another sprig, this time with two nuts. In the fourth, a wheatsheaf. In R J Fletcher's 1901 book *A Short History of Hazel Grove*, the author explains the lion as being from the arms of the Bramhall family and the five nuts in reference to the five parishes: Bramhall, Bosden, Norbury, Offerton and Torkington. The wheatsheaf is from the Chester arms, the hazel, of course, alluding to the name.

HEDON (Yorkshire)

The 1894 edition of *The Book of Pubic Arms* shows the town's seal, a ship at sea with two crew and flags charged with crosses. Hedon was once, before the inlet connecting it to the River Humber dried up, an important port.

HELSTON (Cornwall)

Mentioned, but unillustrated, in both editions of *The Book of Pubic Arms* is the town's seal. The following description is, however, provided: 'St Michael, his wings expanded, standing in a gateway, the two towers domed, upon the upturned dragon, impaling it with his spear, and bearing upon his left arm an escutcheon of the arms of England...' St Michael is the patron saint of Helston's parish church, the towers recalling an ancient castle that once stood in the town. Illustration from *Borough Seals of the Gothic Period* by Gale Pedrick.

HEMEL HEMPSTEAD (Hertfordshire)

In use for at least two centuries, notes C Wilfrid Scott-Giles in 1933, is a device of a shield bearing the head and shoulders of a man in Tudor costume looking much like Holbein's well known portrait of Henry VIII. The design is thought to recall that it was Henry VIII who granted the town its first charter.

HEMSWORTH (Yorkshire)

The urban district council had a shield divided into two parts, the first being red and charged with the crossed keys and crown from the City of York. The second part of the shield displays bulls' heads, the device of Robert Holgate, Archbishop of York 1545-1555. He was a native of the town, founding a grammar school and hospital there. Above the shield, a mitre cap.

HENDON (Middlesex)

A Holy Lamb was used as a symbol by Hendon Urban District Council and its predecessor since 1879 and was included in the arms granted to the borough of Hendon in 1932.

HENLEY-ON-THAMES (Oxfordshire)

The town seal shows the letter 'H' crowned with a ducal coronet above which are the rays of the sun shining down from behind clouds. Illustration from an

Edwardian postcard. Debrett's *House of Commons* for 1893, however, shows a common seal charged with a lion.

HEREFORD (Herefordshire)

Besieged by the Scots in 1645, the Royalist city of Hereford was thanked for its loyalty by the granting of arms. Here placed around the edge of the shield is a blue border charged with ten saltire crosses representing Scotland's St Andrew. In its centre, the lions of England in silver on a red ground. The thinking here is to suggest that the Royalists were surrounded by the Scots during the siege. The Earl of Levan led the invaders and it is his buckles that we see on the collars of the supporting lions. 'The reward of faithfulness unconquered', reads the motto. Illustration from an Edwardian postcard.

HEREFORDSHIRE

With no arm, records A C Fox-Davies, the county used the three lions from the City of Hereford.

HERNE BAY (Kent)

The use of a heron in the town's heraldry is in reference to its name. We also see in this Edwardian heraldic postcard a representation of the clock tower built from funds provided by Mrs Ann Thwaytes in 1837. The rich widow of a London grocer, Mr Thwaytes was a frequent visitor to Herne Bay between 1834 and 1840. In the distance are the twin towers of the ruined St Mary's Church at Reculver, about three miles east of Herne Bay.

HERTFORD (Hertfordshire)

The town's arms are based on an old seal which shows a hart lodged in water with a tree and triple-towered castle behind. By the Rive Lea, Hertford's castle was built around 911. Illustrations from the 1894 edition of *The Book of Public Arms* and a Wills's cigarette card of 1905.

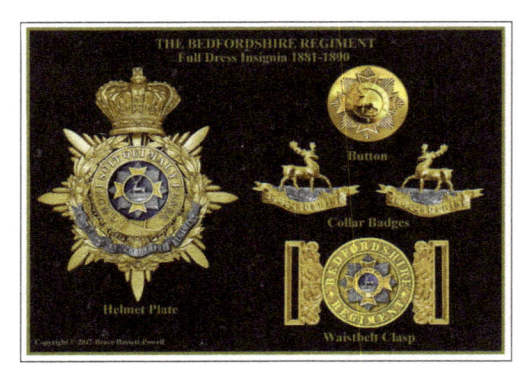

HERTFORDSHIRE

With no arms, records A C Fox-Davies, the county uses those of Hertford. It would not be until 1919 that Hertfordshire was added to the name of the Bedfordshire Regiment, the militia and volunteers of the county having been associated for many years. In recognition, the hart lodged in water was used on many of the badges worn. Illustration courtesy of Uniformology.

50

HESSLE (Yorkshire)

Hessle was well known for its shipbuilding yards which is indicated in the first quarter of the urban district council arms by a three-masted sailing ship. The second quarter has the red rose of York while the third shows a windmill representing the mills used in the manufacture of whiting from local chalk quarries. A fourth quarter is in reference to one of the town's four old gates. Hessle was once the seat of the Suffragan Bishop of Hull and this is indicated by a representation of a bishop's cowl placed in the centre of the four quarters of the shield. Above the shield, a cap of dignity.

HEXHAM (Northumberland)

The town has no arms, notes A C Fox-Davies, but a seal exists consisting of a shield charged with a saltire cross. Built in 674, Hexham Abbey is dedicated to St Andrew. See Northumberland.

HEYTESBURY (Wiltshire)

The seal of the town consists of a long cross mounted on three steps and with a fleur-de-lis on its top. Shields charged with chevrons are placed on each side of the cross. Illustration from the 1915 edition of *The Book of Public Arms*.

HEYWOOD (Lancashire)

The arms show a gold shield charged with five gold roundels and two hollow lozenges. The crest is made up of a falcon holding in its beak a sprig of oak and standing on an uprooted tree trunk. In front of the tree are three gold mascles interlaced. Granted in 1881, the arms were based on those of the Heywood family. 'I fly high', reads the motto. Illustration from the 1915 edition of *The Book of Public Arms*.

HIGHAM FERRERS (Northamptonshire)

Both edition of *The Book of Public Arms* record that the town has no armorial bearings but describes the corporation seal as a left hand couped at the wrist with the little finger and the next doubled in and with the others pointing to the left side giving blessing. Under the hand are nine men's heads couped at the neck.

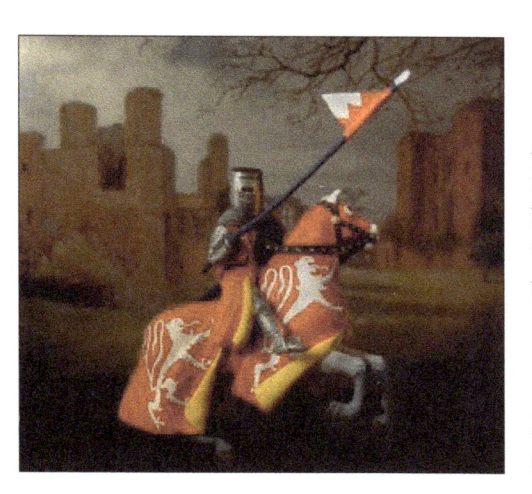

HINCKLEY (Leicestershire)

A simple shield for Hinckley Urban District Council divided into two sections, one silver, one red. This was the device as borne on the banner of Simon de Montifort Earl of Leicester. The illustration shows Simon de Montifort against a backdrop of Kenilworth Castle.

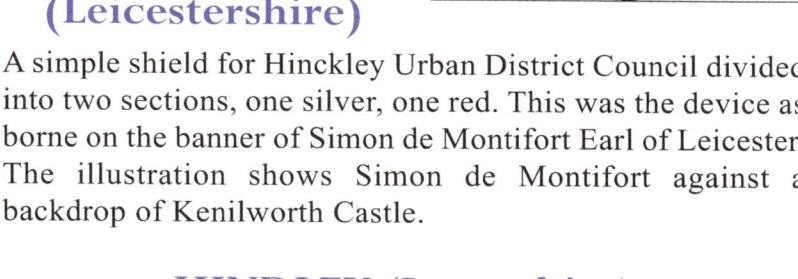

HINDLEY (Lancashire)

Hindley Urban District Council used the device of a hind in allusion to the name.

HOLBORN (London)

Here in the arms granted in 1906 we see references to local churches: the red cross for those of St George-the-Martyr and St George, Bloomsbury, the wounded hind that of St Giles-in-the-Fields and in the crest St Andrew's. Long connected with the borough were the Russells, Dukes of Bedford, the three scallop shells being from that source. Within the area are two Inns of Court, the lion supporter representing the De Lacys, Earls of Lincoln whose house became Lincoln's Inn, while the griffin is from Gray's Inn. In 1905 the tobacco firm of W D & H O Wills published a set of cigarette cards, No 160 of which illustrated a different design. On a shield are featured the three saints and what the notes on the reverse of the card describe as 'the well-known old houses opposite Gray's Inn Road.' Also mentioned as being included in the design are a strawberry garden and a brook. Strawberries, of course, in reference to the remark made by Gloucester in *Richard III*: 'My lord of Ely, when I was last in Holborn, I saw good strawberries in your garden there.' The extensive gardens at Ely Palace were indeed famous for its fruit and flowers, the latter a reminder of the now underground river, the Hole Bourne. 'Many shall pass through, and learning shall be increased', reads the motto.

HONITON (Devonshire)

The seal of the town shows a representation of the Baptism of Christ by St John the Baptist. In the lower part is a sprig of honeysuckle which, according to C W Scott-Giles in his *Civic Arms of England and Wales*, alludes to the name of the town. An alternative explanation could be, however, that the honeysuckle is in reference to the fact that Honiton is famous world-wide for its lace, which specialises in flower designs.

HORBURY (Yorkshire)

On a silver shield, a black diagonal bar charged with three silver towers. Horbury Urban District Council based its arms on those of Sir John de Horbury who was lord of the manor in the fourteenth century.

HORNCHURCH (Essex)

A silver shield charged with a red saltire cross between three red roses, at the bottom a red heart and on the cross, a silver martlet. Above the shield is a bull's head. The roses are from the heraldry of William de Wykeham, a local land owner, the heart from that of Bernard of Savoy and the martlet from Edward the Confessor who had historical links with the area. St Andrew's is the parish church, which explains the saltire cross, and the bull's head, it is thought, is in reference to a stone carving there. This, perhaps, the origins of the town's name.

HORNSEY (London)

The arms shown were granted to this Middlesex, north London district in 1904, the image being from a postcard published in the following year. This part of London was in ancient times covered by vast forests, the two uprooted trees recalling that. The swords are those of St Paul and represent the See of London which once held the Manor of Hornsey. 'The better prepared, the stronger', reads the motto.

HORSEFORTH (Yorkshire)

The urban district council used the device of a horse in allusion to its name.

HORSHAM (Sussex)

A lion rampant resting its right hind foot on the letter 'H'. The lion, notes C W Scott-Giles, is probably that of the De Braose family who once held the manor.

HORWICH (Lancashire)

The arms assumed by Horwich Urban District Council consisted of a shield charged with a running deer, a gold crown around its neck, supported by two foresters with bows. During the Middle Ages Horwich began as a hunting chase used by the barons of Manchester. Foresters were appointed to deter illegal hunting.

HOVE (Sussex)

Here in the arms granted to the town in 1899 we see a saltire cross in reference to the old parish church of St Andrew, a pair of leg irons remembering the close-by Aldrington's St Leonard's Church, chequers from the arms of the De Warenne family and the three birds used by Hove on its ancient seal before it obtained arms. The border is charged with the martlets of Sussex. The ship crest represents a French galley and commemorates the many attacks on the coast at Hove during the sixteenth century. Illustration from a postcard posted in 1905.

HUCKNALL (Nottinghamshire)

The shield of the urban district council is divided into quarters, the first and fourth having three red diagonal lines on a silver ground. This device represents a connection with the Byron family who had property in close-by Newstead. In the second and third quarters, each has a boar's head surrounded by three stars. This, explains C Wilfrid Scott-Giles, seems to be 'an erroneous version of the arms of Gordon of Gight.' George Gordon was the maternal grandfather of poet Lord Byron who is buried at the parish church of Hucknall.

HUDDERSFIELD (Yorkshire)

Debrett's *House of Commons* in 1874 shows arms made up of a shield charged with a central bar. There are two boars above the bar, one below and a fourth serving as a crest. A C Fox-Davies records in 1894 the arms shown in the second illustration. The rams upon the shield and the ram's head in the crest are an allusion to the fact that the freehold of the town has almost exclusively belonged to the Ramsden family. The towers, notes R Bretton in his booklet on West Riding civic heraldry, 'doubtless refer to Castle Hill upon which a castle was built by King Stephen or by Ilbert de Laci, the Norman lord of the manor.' The ram crest, with its sprig from a cotton tree, is in reference to Huddersfield's wool and cotton industries. Illustration from a postcard posted in 1904.

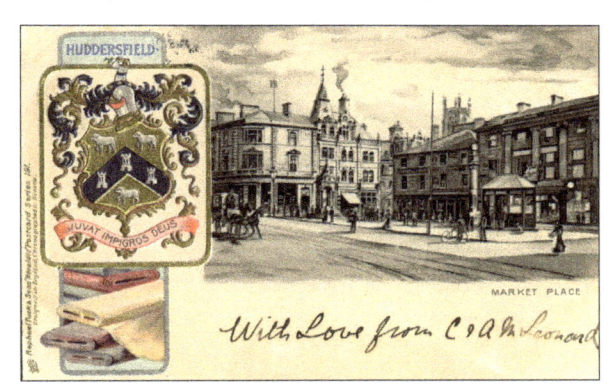

HULL (Yorkshire)

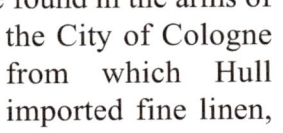

The gold crowns on a blue ground. C W Scott-Giles offers three explanations regarding the use of the crowns. Tradition has it that a local company of merchant adventurers had likened themselves to the three Kings of the East who followed the star to Bethlehem and used the crowns as a device. More likely, he notes, the origin may be found in the arms of the City of Cologne from which Hull imported fine linen, and even more likely a reference to Edward I. The king had recognised the then town of Wykeham-upon-Hull as an important port and in giving it a charter changed its name to King's Town. Kingston-Upon-Hull, of course, is now the full name. An ancient seal shows the figure of a king with a lion on either side, a third at his foot. The illustrations are from a Wills's cigarette card of 1905 and Gale Pedrick's *Borough Seals of the Gothic Period*.

HUNTINGDON (Huntingdonshire)

A stag is being chased by two hounds belonging to a huntsman who is armed with bow and arrow and blows a horn—a hunting scene in allusion, of course, to the name. He is thought to be Robin Hood, that taker from the rich and giver to the poor, outlaw often identified as none other than the Earl of Huntingdon himself. In the centre of the device is a tree which has on its right side a bird (no doubt not to be the hunted on this occasion) balanced on one of its lower branches. Illustrated is an old seal of the birthplace of Oliver Cromwell taken from the 1894 edition of *The Book of Public Arms*. Around the edge the date 1628, the year Cromwell became Member of Parliament for Huntingdon.

HUNTINGDONSHIRE

A C Fox-Davies notes that the county has no armorial bearings but mentions a seal identical to that of Huntingdon with the exception that the date instead reads 1889, the year in which under the Local Government Act 1888 Huntingdonshire became an administrative county.

HYDE (Cheshire)

The manorial family of Hyde (Sir Nicholas became Chief Justice of England, Robert making a name for himself as attorney-general to Anne of Denmark) are represented in the lower portion of the shield. In the chief, other devices are relevant to local industries: a hatters' bow, cog-wheel, miners' picks and Davy lamp. The crest too shows how local people of the town were employed. Here, in blue and with a gold lozenge pattern, is a bundle of cotton prints, a sprig from a cotton tree and a shuttle. Illustration from *The Arms of Cheshire* by John N C Lewis.

54

HYTHE (Kent)

The seal of the town, one of the Cinque Ports, bears a one-masted ship at sea with a crew of four men, one blowing a horn, two perched on the yardarm. In the sea are seven fish which possibly are in allusion to the two so-called Ancient Towns (Rye and Winchelsea) associated with the Cinque Ports. Illustration from the 1894 edition of *The Book of Public Arms*.

ILCHESTER (Somersetshire)

Within a crescent, an estoile of sixteen points, the badge of King John. Illustration from the 1894 edition of *The Book of Public Arms*.

ILFRACOMBE (Devonshire)

The shield of the arms assumed by Ilfracombe Urban District Council was divided into quarters, the first being black with a silver bar between three silver battleaxes. These are from the Wrey family. The second quarter, with its six single-masted ships, is in reference to the six that were supplied by Ilfracombe for Edward III's wars in France. From the Bourchier family, a red engrained cross appears in the third quarter which is in company with four black water budgets, the fourth having an oar placed upon blue wavy lines representing water. This from the seal of the old Local Board of Health. Still with the sea, the supporters take the form of two dolphins. Both the Wreys and Bourchiers were former lords of the manor.

ILKESTON (Derbyshire)

Coal mining, iron working, lace and glove making were the main industries of the town. The Stanton Ironworks was a major employer; the symbol of Mars (seen on the crest and in the centre of the shield) represents this. The bear's head holds a miners' lamp in its mouth. Here too is a representation of Maltese lace, gloves and hanks of cotton. 'Labour overcomes all things', reads the motto. Illustration from the 1915 edition of *The Book of Public Arms*.

IPSWICH (Suffolk)

With a strong connection to the sea, the town shows on its arms granted in 1561, seahorse supporters, a shield based on that of the Cinque Ports with its half-ship hulks, and a ship. The latter was a feature on a thirteenth-century seal. Illustrations from an Edwardian postcard and Gale Pedrick's *Borough Seals of the Gothic Period*.

ISLE OF MAN

The three legs in armour flexed at the knee are said to have been adopted as arms by three thirteenth-century kings of the Isle of Man. Translated, the motto more or less announces 'Whithersoever you throw it, it will stand.' There is, of course, the thought that the Isle of Man 'kneels to England, kicks at Scotland and spurns Ireland'.

ISLINGTON (London)

Arms were granted to the borough in 1901 and shown in its shield are the emblems symbolic of Islington's four manors: a crutched cross (Knights Hospitaller of St John of Jerusalem), Highbury (the lion), Canonbury (eagle) and Barnsbury (a water bouget). Water bougets (or water buckets) were leather bags or bottles carried in twos on a yoke over the shoulder. Another can be seen in the crest together with a longbow representing Islington's connection with archery. Illustration from the 1915 edition of *The Book of Public Arms*.

JARROW (Durham)

The arms granted in 1930 replaced the unauthorised design shown in the Edwardian postcard illustrated. Here, and representing the town's shipbuilding industry, is a sailing ship at sea. It was Charles Mark Palmer who established a shipyard at Jarrow in 1852 where he became the first manufacturer of armour plate in the world. Two of the crowns in the first quarter of the shield are navel crowns, the church in the second being a representation of the monastery founded in 681 in which the Venerable Bede wrote his famous book. The crest is that of Charles Palmer. 'By labour and science', translates the motto.

KEIGHLEY (Yorkshire)

The black line across the centre of the shield (a fess in heraldry) and the red dragon's head crest are both from the arms of the Keighley family who were for many generations lords of the manor. When one of them in Queen Elizabeth's day married a Cavendish, this brought the serpent and stags' heads to the arms and here we see both in those of the borough, granted in 1883. The town's industry owes much to the well-watered valley in which it stands, and this is remembered by the two wavy-lined circles (they represent fountains in heraldry) seen on the fess and crest. About ten miles in length, the River Worth passes Keighley before it joins the Aire, thus explaining the motto.

KENDAL (Westmorland)

A C Fox-Davies notes that Kendal has no armorial bearings but mentions a seal which he thinks represents a view of the town. Certainly his 1894 *The Book of Public Arms* illustration shows a cluster of buildings with possibly a church at one end, and separately a castle with two towers and a central dome. All around are birds. He then tells of a coat of arms that he had been sent to him which 'defies description' and is content with simply mentioning that it consists of a shield divided into four sections and with two unidentified devises. There is a motto, *'Pannus mihi panis'*, which translates as Wool is my bread. It would seem that C Wilfrid Scott-Giles was better informed and states in his 1933 edition of *Civic Heraldry* that the unidentified charges are wool hooks and teazles, both essential tools in the woollen industry which had been important to the town since the fourteenth century. He also goes on to say that the arms, although not registered with the Heralds, had been in use since at least 1629. Returning to the seal illustrated, Kendal was at one time referred to as Kirkby in Kendal which explains the initial letters 'KK'. By authority of the queen, the seal was obtained in 1576.

KENILWORTH (Warwickshire)

The seal of the council shows a view of the keep at Kenilworth Castle. Of Norman origins, the castle had withstood a six-month siege in 1266 which is thought to have been the longest in medieval English history.

KENSINGTON (London)

Granted in 1901, the arms of this London borough are divided into four quarters. Sharing the top left quarter with the crown and fleur-de-lis of the Virgin Mary, to whom the parish church is dedicated, is the star from the De Veres who held the manor from the eleventh to the sixteenth century. The Abbey of Abingdon latter took part of the manor and this is recalled by its arms (top right) and the bishops mitre (bottom right). The final quarter (bottom left) shows the red roses of Sir Walter Cope, who moved into the manor in 1610, and the cross of Sir Henry Rich who took over the property having married the heiress of the Copes, Isabel. He became the 1st Baron Kensington. Illustration from a 1905 Ja-Ja postcard.

KENT

Both editions note that the county has no armorial bearings, but certainly in use was the familiar white horse on a red ground as illustrated in the 1894 edition of *The Book of Public Arms*.

KESWICK (Cumberland)

The seal of the urban district council showed a view of mountains together with a motto taken from Psalm 121, 'The hills whence cometh my help.' Keswick owed much to its early copper mining. A profitable material now called graphite was also discovered which went to make pencils, an industry that would make the town famous. The seal seems to be all that is recorded heraldically in the several reference books consulted. There exists, however, an Edwardian postcard and the crested china item illustrated both of which show a shield charged with a ship on water and a canton displaying a diagonal line.

KIDDERMINSTER (Worcestershire)

The Corporation of Kidderminster had not obtained arms, but both editions of *The Book of Public Arms* note that those in regular use have two gold chevrons, each with four black roundels, and a further three on the shield, this time in gold. All are placed on a blue ground. The motto translates as 'With God's help, it flourishes by art and industry'. C Wilfrid Scott-Giles gives the explanation that the chevrons and gold roundels are from the arms of the Kyderminster family and that the black are possibly from roundels in the arms of the See of Worcester. Certainly the town's main trade of carpet making would qualify as both art and industry.

KIDSGROVE (Staffordshire)

A C Fox-Davies noted that there were no armorial bearings, but a landscape showing three young goats (kids) in a grove of trees had been placed upon an shield and attributed to the town. A pun on the name, of course.

57

KING'S LYNN (Norfolk)

The heads of three gold dragons each appearing to be swallowing gold crosses. It is thought that these charges refer to the legend of St Margaret of Antioch to whom the parish church is dedicated. Having been imprisoned for her beliefs, Margaret was devoured by the Devil who had taken the form of a dragon. But the power of a cross she was wearing burst the creature open allowing Margaret to emerge from its body unhurt. A pelican serves as a crest which is said to represent a Christian emblem, the bird being the symbol of the Eucharist.

KINGSTON-UPON-THAMES (Surrey)

Fishing was once so important to the town (the Doomsday Book mentioning that it had three salmon fisheries) that it placed three salmon on its arms. Here they are displayed on a postcard posted in 1907. In the 1893 edition of Debrett's *House of Commons* the fish are shown in company with three lions and the letter 'R', the latter, possibly in reference to the fact that Kingston was included in the Sessional Division of Richmond.

KNARESBOROUGH (Yorkshire)

Both editions of *The Book of Public Arms* refer to the seal and describe it as having a castle, a scroll bearing the letters 'ERQR' and a left hand in armour holding a branch of acorns. There is also the date '1611'. A C Fox-Davies provides no illustration, but an Edwardian postcard shows arms which differ slightly to what the author described for the seal.

KNUTSFORD (Cheshire)

The seal of the urban district council showed a man wearing a crown wading in water and with a battleaxe over his shoulder. Could this be King Knut, Canute as we better know him? The producers of the Edwardian postcard illustrated obviously thought so.

LAMBETH (London)

It is not until the 1915 edition of *The Book of Public Arms* that Lambeth is mentioned, A C Fox-Davies noting that the borough has no arms. He includes no illustration but describes, however, the seal in use as follows: '…two escutcheons, the one of the Archiepiscopal; See of Canterbury, the other the Duchy of Cornwall, below these a lamb passant on a mount and underneath the word Hythe.' Richard Crosley in his book *London's Coats of Arms and the Stories They Tell* records that the seal was designed and brought into use at the beginning of 1901. Of the Cornwall shield, this is relevant as a large part of the borough belongs to the Duchy of Cornwall while that of the See remembers the Archbishops of Canterbury who have been resident at Lambeth Palace since the thirteenth century. Lambeth was once known as Lambhythe, which explains the inclusion of the lamb and word. In the Edwardian postcard illustrated the letters 'VR' and the date 1900 have been included.

LANCASHIRE

The 1894 edition of *The Book of Public Arms* states that the county has no official arms but those in use are described and illustrated: three lions and a label on a shield accompanied by a talbot holding a feather in its paw on either side and a crown above. Talbots are dogs similar to a Labrador. But having been granted in 1903, arms are shown in 1915 as follows: With a red ground, a shield is divided into three pointed sections referred to in heraldry as piles, each being charged with a red rose. The same shield appears on both of the supporters and as part of the crest. The lions are from the arms of the Ferrers, Earls of Derby, who held the land between the Rivers Ribble and Mersey during the thirteenth century. The motto translates as 'In council is wisdom'.

LANCASTER (Lancashire)

C Wilfrid Scott-Giles records that the arms were 'clearly suggested by the arms and badge of Edmund, first Earl of Lancaster' who had the lions of England together with the fleurs-de-lis of France. In the motto, 'Loyne' is a form of Lune, the river on which Lancaster stands and takes its name.

LAUNCESTON (Cornwall)

Launceston Castle, it is thought, was most likely built by Robert the Count of Mortain after 1068. Originally in wood, it was reconstructed in stone during the twelfth century and like a three-tier cake perches high above the town. The lion in the crest is that from the arms of Richard, Earl of Cornwall, the ostrich feathers those of the Prince of Wales, Duke of Cornwall. The arms were granted in 1573. Illustrations are from the 1915 edition of *The Book of Public Arms* and a Wills's cigarette card of 1905.

LEAMINGTON (Warwickshire)

Here we find a green lion with two tails representing Dudley, Earl of Warwick, the chevron placed over its body is from the Fisher family, the red stars from Willes and the fleur-de-lis those of the De Clintons. Leamington is well known for its health-giving waters and the arms remember this by including the Rod of Æsculapius as its crest. Also seen is the ragged staff of the Earls of Warwick. The motto translates as 'Only those that are honourable are good'. Illustration from an Edwardian postcard.

LEEDS (Yorkshire)

English historian and writer of *Britannia* wrote of Leeds in 1590 that it was '…rendered wealthy by its woollen manufacturers', so it comes as no surprise that a golden fleece features in the arms recorded by the Heralds in 1662. Owls, three of them, are from the arms of the Saville family, the motto translating as 'For King and Law'. The illustrations are from a Faulkner postcard of 1905, and show the cap badge worn by the 15th (Service) Battalion (1st Leeds) of the Prince of Wales's Own (West Yorkshire Regiment) during the Great War.

LEEK (Staffordshire)

'Supported by skill, there is no cause for despair' reads the motto of the of the Leek Urban District Council. It also shows the Rod of Mercury, which is a symbol of commerce, and bales of goods. The town's economy was greatly centered around its textile mills, silk working in particular. There exists a commercial half-penny token dated 1793 that bears the rod and bales of goods.

LEICESTER (Leicestershire)

A red shield charged with a silver cinquefoil, the crest being a wyvern, the motto *'Semper Eadem'*. These were the arms granted in 1619, the cinquefoil having come from the arms of Robert FitzPernell, Earl of Leicester. The wyvern was the crest of Thomas of Lancaster, second Lancastrian Earl of Leicester. The motto is that of Elizabeth I.

LEICESTERSHIRE

A C Fox-Davies notes in both editions of his *Book of Public Arms* that the county has no armorial bearings and that the arms of Leicester are usually employed. He also mentions that those of Lord Howe, the Lord Lieutenant of Leicestershire have, on occasion been used. The county council seal showed a view of an embattled and ruined gateway within the inscription *'Sigillum comitatis Leicestriae Councillii'*.

LEIGH (Lancashire)

The arms granted in 1899 include heraldry from local families. Here we have the spearhead of the Urmestones of Westleigh, the star of the Bradshaws, a shuttle of the Shuttleworths and a sparrowhawk from the heraldry of the Athertons. The bear's paw is from the crest of Lord Lilford. 'To hasten with equal foot', translates the motto.

LEIGHTON BUZZARD (Bedfordshire)

The urban district council used the arms and crest of the Bossard family: on a red ground a gold saltire cross and blue star. Above this a black crowned eagle on gold, the crest the same.

LEOMINSTER (Herefordshire)

The seal shows a representation of St Peter to whom, with St Paul, the parish church is dedicated. Although no arms were recorded by the Heralds' College the corporation did use the device of a red lion rampant on a gold shield. The lion holds in its left forepaw a horned lamb which gives reference to the woollen industry once important to the town for several centuries. It has been suggested that the use of the lion was in allusion to the first three letters of the town's name.

LEWES (Sussex)

The chequers seen on the arms of this Sussex town were derived from those of the Warennes, Earls of Surrey, who held the barony of Lewes from the Conquest until the fourteenth century. Heraldically, the top right-hand corner of the shield is described as a canton charged with a lion rampant among cross-crosslets and their source draws two thoughts: from the arms of the De Braose or Mowbrays. The illustration is of a Town Band bass drum on show at Lewes Museum.

LEWISHAM (London)

The gold device seen in the first quarter of the shield is a representation of a dagger and reputed to be, notes Richard Crosley in his *London Coats of Arms and the Stories They Tell,* from the arms of King Alfred, first Lord of the Manor of Lewisham. Below this, the stag's head is from the heraldry of Lord Dartmouth, also Lord of the Manor at one time, and opposite we see the bear's head from that of Lord Northbrook who held Lee. That leaves the second quarter which reminds us that Lewisham was once part of Kent. Lord Dartmouth again in the left supporter, and Lord Northbrook's bear serves as that on the right. A raven, which refers to the River Ravensbourne, forms the crest, the motto translating as 'The welfare of the people is the highest law'.

LICHFIELD (Staffordshire)

The arms illustrated are as recorded by A C Fox-Davies in both his 1894 and 1915 editions of *The Book of Public Arms*. C Wilfrid Scott-Giles notes that the chevrons were most likely derived from the heraldry of the ancient family of Stafford. I have two editions (1874 and 1893) of Debrett's *House of Commons* to hand and both show a design of three armoured men who seem to have arms or legs missing. All around are weapons, swords and an axe, a crown and flag. The scene is, in fact, from the Lichfield seal granted in 1548 and recalls the story of how in around 300AD about a thousand Christians were massacred by a Roman army and their bodies left unburied.

LINCOLN (Lincolnshire)

On a silver shield, a red cross charged with a gold fleur-de-lis, Debrett's *House of Commons* showing this together with a castle entrance as the city's common seal. A seal is also on record which featured a representation of the Blessed Virgin. Lincoln's castle was built during the latter part of the eleventh century by William the Conqueror, the work beginning on its cathedral, dedicated to the Blessed Virgin Mary, in 1072.

LINCOLNSHIRE

The county, notes A C Fox-Davies, has no armorial bearings and used those of the City of Lincoln.

LISKEARD (Cornwall)

A C Fox-Davies notes that the town has no armorial bearings but illustrates in his 1894 edition of *The Book of Public Arms* its seal: a fleur-de-lis with two birds perched upon it. Above, two rings below two feathers. C W Scott-Giles notes that the feathers are those of the Prince of Wales, the rings possibly intended to represent the roundels from the arms of the Duchy of Cornwall.

LITTLE HULTON (Lancashire)

The urban district council's quartered shield, notes C Wilfrid Scott-Giles, was made up of the arms of local landowners at the time the Local Board was formed in 1872: the Duke of Bridgewater (first and fourth quarters), Lord Kenyon (second), Mr Robert Fletcher (third). The Fletchers of Peel Hall were important landowners and coal producers.

LITTLE LEVER (Lancashire)

The cock crows and a bugle sounds. Two good systems of alarm calls and a possible pun on the name of Lever from whose arms come the crest used by the Little Lever Urban District Council. Also from that family comes the shield with its two black diagonal bars on a silver ground. 'I scorn either to change or fear', translates the motto.

LITTLE YARMOUTH (Norfolk)

A silver shield charged with a black chevron between three black seals' feet. Seals and the spectacle they provide draw visitors to Little Yarmouth and the Norfolk coast,

LIVERPOOL (Lancashire)

Liverpool's arms were granted in 1797, the famous 'Liver Bird' making three appearances: on the shield, the banner held by the left supporter, and as the crest. They are cormorants, each holding firmly in its beak a branch of laver (seaweed). With its important association with the sea, it comes as no surprise to find that Liverpool's supporters are none other than Neptune (left) and Triton who blows a shell and holds a banner charged with a sailing ship. 'God hath granted us the sea', translates the motto.

LONDON (CITY OF)

The 'Square Mile', its arms showing the red cross of St George and the sword of St Paul, the patron saint of London who according to legend was beheaded with that weapon. But we must not believe the popular idea that the dagger-like short sword was that used by Sir William Walworth to stab Wat Tyler in Smithfield on 15 June 1381. The device was, in fact, in use many years before the rebellious Tyler met his end. With St George must come dragons and here we see a wing as a crest and the creatures in full as supporters. The postcard illustrated was posted in October 1907.

LONDON COUNTY COUNCIL

The council's arms were granted by Royal Warrant dated 29 July 1914 and show the River Thames in its silver and blue wavy lines. We also have the cross of St George and the lion of England.

LONG EATON (Derbyshire)

The urban district council used a hart lodged in a field within park railings from the insignia of Derby.

LONGTON (Staffordshire)

A C Fox-Davies illustrates the complex arms used by the town in his 1894 edition of *The Book of Public Arms*. He notes in his description how the borough had assumed the shield of the late John Edensor Heathcote, JP of Longton Hall who had died in 1869. 'Somebody else's crest (? That of the Mosley family) was appropriated and the supporters invented.' The latter undoubtably refers to the potteries and local mines.

LOSTWITHIEL (Cornwall)

The seal has a shield charged with a castle rising out of water between two thistles. There are fish in the water and above the shield is the date 1732. The Norman Restormel Castle lies by the River Fowey close to Lostwithiel.

LOUGHBOROUGH (Leicestershire)

Arms were granted on 10 April 1889 which had a gold shield parted by a black bar upon which was placed two gold escallop shells and the device, also gold, referred to in heraldry as a fret. In the top right corner of the shield another term of heraldry, a maunch which is a representation of a sleeve from a women's dress. The lower corner has a black bull's head. The fret and maunch appear again, this time as part of a golden lion crest. 'Victory in truth', translates the motto. Several families long associated with Loughborough are represented: the maunch and bull's head from the heraldry of Hastings, the fret and escallops those of Le De Spencer, the lion for Beaumont.

LOUTH (Lincolnshire)

A C Fox-Davies tells in both his *Book of Public Arms* volumes of correspondence between himself and the Town Clerk of Louth in which he requested an impression of the corporation's seal. The clerk returned the letter stating that 'We have none.' Another source, however, records that with no arms the town uses those of the Louth family: a gold wolf on a black ground. In Debrett's *House of Commons* for 1893, however, there is an image shown under the heading of 'East Lindsey, or Louth' and this shows an amusing scene in which a schoolmaster is beating a pupil as others look on. This, in fact, is the seal of the Edward VI Grammar School, Louth.

LOWESTOFT (Suffolk)

A C Fox-Davies mentions in his 1894 edition of *The Book of Public Arms* that Lowestoft has no armorial bearings, but a seal is in use which shows St Margaret supporting in front of herself a shield charged with a rose and holding over the rose and between her hands an imperial crown. But on 14 February 1913 arms were granted comprising a silver shield charged with a black chevron, two red roses, an antique crown and a blazing sun. On the chevron, and in silver, representations of three plates. The crown recalls that Lowestoft was anciently part of a royal manor, the plates representing the porcelain factory on Crown Street which operated between 1757-1802. For the crest, St Margaret again, identified by the pearl that she holds, to whom the parish church is dedicated.

LUDLOW (Shropshire)

The blue shield of Ludlow is charged with the three white roses and white lion of the Mortimers, Earls of March. A porcupine divided gold and blue forms the crest, C Wilfrid Scott-Giles suggesting that this was most likely derived from the crest of Sir Henry Sidney, President of the Welsh Marches and who died at Ludlow in 1586.

LUGGERSHALL (Wiltshire)

A castle on a blue ground. Luggershall castle, now in ruins, was built during the late eleventh century

LUTON (Bedfordshire)

With King James of Scotland came a group of straw plaiters who settled under the protection of Sir Robert Napier of Luton Hoo in Bedfordshire. This would be the beginning of Luton's most famous industry, hat making. In the town's arms we see a rose from the Napier arms, a thistle remembering the origins of the original straw plaiters, ears of wheat which come from the arms of John Whethamsteade, the Abbot of St Albans who built Luton's St Mary's Church. The beehive represents again, the plaiters, the bees, of course, industry. Luton's arms were granted on 25 July 1876.

LYDD (Kent)

On a blue ground, a silver church with a golden ship behind it rises from the sea. On the ship a man stands blowing a horn, the top left corner of the shield displaying a red cross and four lions. Based on a thirteenth-century seal, the illustration shows an early representation of All Saints, the parish church of Lydd. The town, once part of the Cinque Ports, now stands some three miles from the sea.

LYME REGIS (Dorsetshire)

As a medieval port once of great importance, we see in the ancient seal of the borough a ship of one mast, the mainyard lowered and the mainsail furled. There is a figurehead of a dragon's head at each end, a flag at the masthead charged with a cross, a banner bearing the arms of England and another displaying the arms of Castile and Leon. To the left of the ship there is a representation of the Crucifixion with St John the Evangelist and the Blessed Virgin situated at the foot and to the right St Michael the Archangel and the dragon. In the sky there is the sun, a crescent and star. Gale Pedrick in his *Borough Seals* points out that the inclusion of the arms of Leon and Castile point to the fact that the revenues of the port were included in the dowry of his queen. The Crucifixion, he suggests, is in reference to Glastonbury Abbey. St Michael is the patron saint of Lyme Regis. The second illustration is a detail from a 1905 Ja-Ja postcard.

LYMINGTON (Hampshire)

Lymington's seal dates from the fifteenth century and shows a one-masted ship and the shield from the arms of the Courtenays, the ancient Lords of the Manor.

LYTHAM (Lancashire)

As the arms suggest, Lytham owes much to the sea. In the second quarter of the shield we have a reminder of an industry that was the mainstay of the town's economy for centuries, shrimping. But the sea also brought the tourists and those keen to enjoy a healthy climate. Here too in the arms is the rose of Lancaster and the armoured arm holding a dagger from the heraldry of Lytham's most important family, the Cliftons of Lytham Hall.

MACCLESFIELD (Cheshire)

A rampant lion holding a garb and the motto *'Nec virtus nec copia desunt'* (Neither virtue nor plenty are lacking). C Wilfrid Scott-Giles suggests that the lion is that of the Ferrers, Earls of Derby.

MAIDENHEAD (Berkshire)

The town's name, not from a young lady's head, but from the riverside area where a new wharf or 'Maiden Hythe' was built in early Saxon times. The illustration is from A C Fox-Davies's 1894 edition of *The Book of Public Arms*.

MAIDSTONE (Kent)

The illustration is a detail from a 1905 Ja-Ja postcard, the roundels on the shield being from the Archbishop Courtenay, for who we must thank for Maidstone's All Saints Church, the lion representing England.

MALDENS AND COOMBE (Surrey)

A beehive with several bees flying about it is used by the urban district council.

MALDON (Essex)

There exists an old town seal dated 1682 showing a ship at sea on the obverse and a shield charged with three lions on the reverse. The lions are also seen on a banner flown from the stern of the ship. Also illustrated, and from *Borough & County Arms of Essex* by W Gurney Benham, is the arms as recorded at the College of Arms in 1614 and 1664.

MALMESBURY (Wiltshire)

The town seal has a representation of the castle built by Roger, Bishop of Sarum during the reign of Henry I. Here too at the base of the castle is water (Malmesbury stands on the River Avon), stalks bearing each three ears of wheat, a star and crescent.

MALTON (Yorkshire)

The arms are a punning device on the town's name, two ears of barley for malt and three tuns (a large vat or vessel). In the 1933 edition of *Civic Arms of England and Wales*, the author notes that Malton Urban District Council uses the former arms of Marquesses of Rockingham, the Earls and Barons of Malton.

MANCHESTER (Lancashire)

The arms granted in 1842 show the red lower half of a shield charged with three gold bars (bendlets) in reference to the Byron family. Above this (in the chief), a three-masted ship about which A C Fox-Davies askes the question, 'Was the chief a prophecy of the ship canal?' This may have been the case, remarks C Wilfrid Scott-Giles, 'for although the canal was not opened until 1894 it was projected much earlier.' Designs were in fact prepared in 1840, two years before the arms were granted. The crest is a representation of the terrestrial globe charged with seven bees representing world-wide industry over the seven seas, and the supporters are a silver antelope (from the arms of the Duke of Manchester) and a gold lion. The second illustration (courtesy of Bruce Bassett Powell/Bob Bennett/Uniformology.com) shows how the Manchester Regiment used the arms as a centre to its helmet plates.

MANSFIELD (Nottinghamshire)

In the centre of the arms granted in 1892 is a gold cross representing Edward the Confessor in whose reign the town stood as a royal manor. The cross is placed on a shield quartered black and blue, the first and fourth black quarters being charged with a silver stag's head, the second and third with representations of cotton hanks. A stag's head is from the heraldry of Cavendish-Bentinck, the cotton in reference to local industry. The crest takes the form of an oak tree in front of which are two silver cross-crosslets between two gold stars. Sherwood Forest is represented by the tree, the crosslets being from the arms of Howard, the stars those of Murray, Earl of Mansfield. The motto translates as 'Industry flourishes like the oak'.

MARGATE (Kent)

The arms granted in 1858 display a divided red and blue shield charged with a silver chevron. Above the chevron a gold half-lion-half-ship (Margate was once connected with the Cinque Ports), and below a horse from the arms of Kent. The crest showed a seahorse supporting a ship's mast. The town's industry has long been associated with the sea and as a holiday resort, the choice of motto translating as 'A gate of the sea and heaven and health'.

MARKET HARBOROUGH (Leicestershire)

C Wilfrid Scott-Giles notes in his 1933 edition of *Civic Arms of England and Wales* that Market Harborough Urban District Council uses the arms of the extinct Earldom of Harborough: on a silver shield, a red chevron and three roundels. The crest shows a peacock's tail bound with a gold and red ribbon, the supporters being two silver rams with gold horns and hooves.

MARLBOROUGH (Wiltshire)

C Wilfrid Scott-Giles notes that Marlborough's original arms were a silver tower on a blue ground. Here we see it in the arms illustrated. The other emblems included are said to be 'in commemoration of the duty and homage heretofore said and done by the burgesses and community to the mayor for the time being, his aldermen and brethren of the said town, at the receiving of the oath by any burgess by them admitted, at which time they do present to the mayor a leash of white greyhounds, one white bull and two white capons.'

MELCOMBE REGIS (Dorsetshire)

The common seal, notes Gale Pedrick in *Borough Seals of the Gothic Period*, probably dates from the reign of Edward I and shows an ancient ship between two shields, each charged with a lion rampant and a triple-towered castle. The ship draws attention to the maritime importance of the town, whilst the shield, that of Leon and Castile, indicates that it formed part of the dowry of Queen Eleanor.

MIDDLESBROUGH (Yorkshire)

On a ground of silver is the blue lion from the arms of Robert de Brus of Skelton, who in the twelfth century founded a priory on ground now held by Middlesbrough. Above, and on a black ground, are three gold ships. The blue lion again appears standing on a mural crown decorated with three black anchors in the crest. Middlesbrough's location on the south bank of the River Tees gave rise to a strong connection with the sea via its shipbuilding activities.

MIDDLESEX

On red ground, three seaxes and a gold Saxon crown. These were the arms assigned to the ancient Kingdom of the Middle and East Saxons.

MIDDLETON (Lancashire)

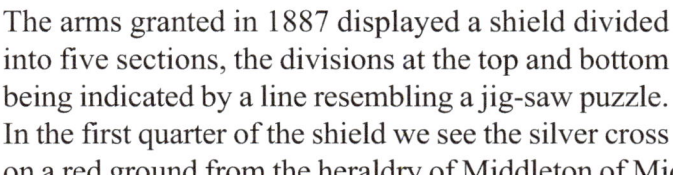

The arms granted in 1887 displayed a shield divided into five sections, the divisions at the top and bottom being indicated by a line resembling a jig-saw puzzle. In the first quarter of the shield we see the silver cross on a red ground from the heraldry of Middleton of Middleton Hall, the second having a black mullet star from the Asheton family. Local industries are represented by a silkworm moth and three sprigs from a cotton tree. C Wilfrid Scott-Giles in his research for the Middleton arms offers an explanation supplied by the town clerk in reference to the stork in the fourth quarter of the shield. It was included, apparently, to 'represent the desire for the increase of the population.' The crest, with its boars' heads, tower and shield charged with a red lion, refers to other families by the name of Middleton, the shield being that of the Earl of Middleton (Scotland). The motto, 'Strong in difficulties' is his too.

MILBOURNEPORT (Somerset)

A common seal of Milbourneport was mentioned as early as 1432, the one in use in 1626 having a shield with a lion passant gardant with the letter 'R' below.

MORECAMBE (Lancashire)

As the town grew and the railway linked it to Skipton and Bradford, many from Yorkshire settled in the area, a fact represented by the two roses in the Morecambe arms. The illustrations are both from Edwardian postcards.

MORLEY (Yorkshire)

In the arms granted in August 1887 we see several references to local industries—wool, cotton and coal. 'He prospers who labours', translates the motto. (Illustration from the Robert Young Civic Heraldry of England and Wales website.)

MORPETH (Northumberland)

The arms illustrated were granted to this Northumberland town in 1552, the gold castle being a representation of that occupied by the Norman family of De Merlay. The eight gold birds around the edge of the shield are martlets, the background lines being silver and red. 'Dwelling 'twixt woods and rivers', translates the motto, the latter referring to the River Wansbeck which surrounds the town on three sides.

MOSSLEY (Lancashire)

Part of Mossley stood in neighbouring Cheshire and this is symbolized by the sheaf of corn on a blue ground in the centre of the upper section of the shield. Here too are roses for Yorkshire and Lancaster and a cotton plant representing the town's one-time chief industry.

MUCH WENLOCK (Shropshire)

Illustrated is the town's seal which represents a triple canopy, the central figure being a saint crowned with a nimbus, seated and supporting a crucifix. On the left side a crowned figure holds a crosier, that to the right being St George trampling on the dragon. The right-hand shield of the three shown at the base of the canopy is identified as being that of the ancient family of Wenlock.

NANTWICH (Cheshire)

Nantwich Urban District Council used the arms attributed to Malbank, or Malbanus, Barons of Nantwich in the eleventh century: a gold and red shield charged with a black diagonal bar.

NELSON (Lancashire)

Much representing Nelson's cotton and wool industries in the arms granted on 5 May 1891—sprigs from a cotton tree, a fleece, shuttle and the reed hooks used in textile weaving. For the crest, a cock from the Tunstall family who employed many in their mills and factories.

NEW MILLS (Derbyshire)

The urban district council used the device of a stag lodged within palings taken from the Derby arms.

NEW ROMNEY (Kent)

Three gold lions of England on a blue shield. The lions reflect the fact that New Romney was once one of the Cinque Ports.

NEWARK (Nottinghamshire)

Although the town's full name is Newark-upon-Trent, it actually stands on the River Devon close to its junction with the Trent. So strong is the river connection that the arms granted in 1561 made several references: the blue and silver wavy lines, the otter and beaver supporters (granted at a later date) and a cormorant holding in its beak an eel. The upper section of the shield is charged with a fleur-de-lis, lion (both of England) and a peacock. The latter, it is thought, was included as a symbol of town pride. The motto, which translates as 'Trust God and sally', was taken from the words of the mayor to Lord Bellasyse during the siege of Newark by the Parliamentarians in 1646. Illustration from the Robert Young 'Civic Heraldry of England & Wales' website.

NEWBURY (Berkshire)

The seal shows a castle with three towers, a representation of Newbury Castle which held out against King Stephen during a siege of 1152.

NEWCASTLE-UNDER-LYME (Staffordshire)

Illustrated is the town seal which shows a representation of the 'new' castle built in the twelfth century. There are three shields hanging from the battlements: from left to right, those of Henry III, Edmund Earl of Cornwall and Prince Edward Earl of Chester.

NEWCASTLE-UPON-TYNE (Northumberland)

Newcastle owes much of its prosperity to the tidal river upon which it stands, the seahorse supporters representing this. When the arms were granted is not on record, but A C Fox-Davies makes reference to Richardson's 'Table Book' which tells of '…an ancient shield formally placed at the north front of Newgate' which places them as being in use prior to 1390. C Wilfrid Scott-Giles notes that the royal lion and pennon of St George in the crest 'are appropriate to a town which on several occasions during the fourteenth century resisted attacks by the Scots and withstood a siege in the Royalist cause during the Civil War.' 'She bravely defends and triumphs', translates the motto.

NEWPORT (Isle of Wight)
The town's seal dates from the fifteenth century and shows a one-masted ship.

NEWQUAY (Cornwall)
A blue shield charged with a swimming fish. A busy fishing trade existed at Newquay since medieval times.

NEWTON (Lancashire)
A ram's head issuing from a ducal coronet and holding in its mouth a sprig of laurel. This the heraldry of the Legh family who were once resident in the area.

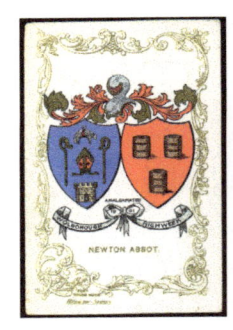

NEWTON ABBOT (Devonshire)
As the Edwardian postcard illustrated shows, Newton Abbot's arms were made up of two shields, one representing Wolborough, the other, Highweek. The 1901 date referes to the formation that year of the Newton Abbot Urban District Council. In the Wolborough shield we see a reference to its association with Tore Abbey, the fleece being a pun of the parish name. The Highweek shield shows representations of three tuns (barrels).

NEWTON-IN-MAKERFIELD (Lancashire)
A silver ram's head with gold horns holding in its mouth a sprig of laurel from the arms of the Legh family.

NEWTOWN (Hampshire)
The town's seal represents an antique ship on the sea with one mast and flying a pennon. The ship is charge with a lion passant, a mullet star, a crescent and the shield of St George.

NORFOLK
Arms were granted to Norfolk County Council in 1904, C Wilfrid Scott-Giles noting that the lower part of the shield is taken from the arms attributed to Ranulf de Guader, the first Earl of Norfolk. The upper sections indicate the royal association with the Norfolk town of Sandringham. Prior to its grant of arms, Norfolk used those of the City of Norwich.

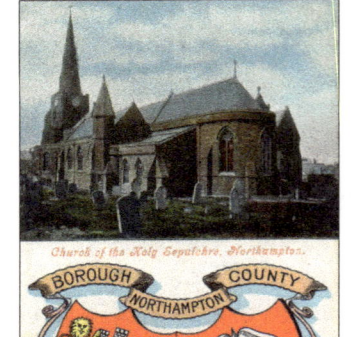

NORTHAMPTON (Northamptonshire)
Here we see the Northampton Castle, which was built by Simon de Senlis around 1100, supported by two lions. The county had no armorial bearings but used a seal showing a rose. In this Edwardian postcard featuring Northampton's Church of the Holy Sepulchre we see both the borough arms and the county seal.

NORTHAMPTONSHIRE
The county has no arms but uses in its seal a rose.

70

NORTHUMBERLAND

Illustrated is the county council seal which incorporates the arms of Northumbria, Berwick, Morpeth, Tynemouth, Corbridge, Hexham and Alnwick.

NORTHWICH (Cheshire)

The seal of Northwich Urban District Council includes the arms of the Earldom of Chester, owners of the manor until 1237, supported by a lion and a sea wolf. A crest takes the form of a steamship, the town prospering much from its exporting of salt.

NORWICH (Norfolk)

A red shield charged with a silver castle and gold lion. Her we have Norwich Castle which was built by King Stephen on the site of an old fortress erected by William I. The lion is said to have been granted by Edward III. In the Wills's cigarette card illustrated we see placed above the shield a representation of a civic fur cap and supporters in the form of two angels with drawn swords.

NOTTINGHAM (Nottinghamshire)

The red shield illustrated was that recorded by the Heralds in 1614, the crest and supporters being granted in June 1898. Here on the shield we have a ragged wooden cross which can be associated with St Helena, but in this case the thoughts are that it represents Sherwood Forest, together with three gold crowns. And who else would be suitable as supporters but Robin Hood himself. That is until 3 November 1908, when that taker from the rich to give to the poor was stood down in favour of two stags. For the crest, a castle of three towers, one with a crescent, another an estoile star. 'Virtue survives death', translates the motto.

NOTTINGHAMSHIRE

The county council has a seal that includes a shield divided into quarters by a ragged cross charged with a crown. In the first quarter is an uprooted tree in reference to Sherwood Forest, the second a selection of tools from the mining industry, the third a lace-making machine and the fourth a wheatsheaf, the latter three representing local industries. The cross and crown are from the City of Nottingham.

NUNEATON (Warwickshire)

Chris J Smith notes in his booklet *The Civic Heraldry of Warwickshire* that the common seal of the borough, before arms were granted in April 1932, showed a view of Nuneaton Priory taken from an old print of around 1730 by Samuel and Nathaniel Buck.

OAKHAM (Rutland)

A black horseshoe on a gold ground. A C Fox-Davies refers to the legend that when Queen Elizabeth I was passing through the town her horse lost a shoe. One was supplied and afterwards the privilege of claiming a horseshoe from any royal personage or nobleman entering the parish was established. The shoes are traditionally affixed to a wall at Castle Hall.

OAKHAMPTON (Devonshire)

The shield is made up of gold and blue chequers with two silver bars, a castle forming the crest. Oakhampton Castle was built between 1068 and 1086 by Baldwin FitzGilbert as a guarding point across the West Okement River.

OLDHAM (Lancashire)

The arms granted in 1894 show a shield divided gold and black. On the lower black section a gold chevron and three owls, the upper gold portion, a red rose between two red rings. Another owl forms the crest. The Oldham family's arms were the inspiration, one notable member being Hugh Oldham who died in 1519 and was Bishop of Exeter. The owls, an illusion to the town and family name, and also lending themselves to the motto *'Sapere aude'* (Dare to be wise).

ORFORD (Suffolk)

On a silver shield, a gold tower on an ancient black ship. There on the coast, Orford during the Middle Ages stood as one of Suffolk's important ports and fishing villages. Orford Castle was built between 1165 and 1173 by Henry II.

OSSETT (Yorkshire)

The town's seal gives reference to its several industries: a factory building, wheatsheaf, a fleece and a pithead. Coal had been mined in the area since the fourteenth century, textile mills employing many both in the manufacture of woollen garments and the recycled material known as shoddy.

OSWESTRY (Shropshire)

The town seal represents a figure of King Oswald crowned and seated on a throne. He holds a sword in one hand and grasps a tree in the other. King of Northumbria from 634 until his death, Oswald met his end during the Battle of Maserfield at Oswestry in 642. His body was dismembered by the Mercians and one of the several legends surrounding the event spoke of the king's right arm being picked up by a bird and taken to an ash tree. The arm fell to the ground and where it landed a spring immediately formed. Both the tree ('Oswald's tree') and spring were soon associated with healing powers. Oswestry also used the arms of a monastery established by Oswald: a red cross on a silver ground charged with four gold lions.

OTLEY (Yorkshire)

Otley Urban District Council obtained arms, notes R Bretton in *West Riding Civic Heraldry,* on 14 December 1951 but had prior to that 'made use for nearly 60 years of the Arms of the Otley Armed Association,' three towers arranged two over one and with crossed keys between the upper two. Armed

72

associations sprang up during the last years of the eighteenth century and were made up of local volunteers. That in Otley was raised in 1798 under the command of Major Commandant William Vavasour, Mr Bretton's in his entry for Otley quoting the following from 'the Grant to the Armed Association': 'The inhabitants of the said town having formed themselves into an Armed Association consisting of Three Companies called The Otley Association…are desirous of bearing upon the Colours of their Corps such armorial ensigns as may have allusion to the three ancient castles of Cawood, Wistow, and Otley by which united denominations the Liberty of Otley, under the Archbishops of York. The towers therefor represent those castles and the keys represent the archbishops and are taken from their Arms.'

OXFORD (Oxfordshire)

On a silver shield, a red ox fording water. The crest a half-lion wearing a crown and holding a Tudor rose. The supporters take the form of an elephant depicted in black with white spots and a silver ear, and a green beaver with a blue and white tail wearing a gold collar. 'Strong is truth', translates the motto. The shield was featured on a fourteenth-century seal. The significance of the elephant is unknown but C Wilfrid Scott-Giles suggests that the beaver represents the River Thames.

OXFORDSHIRE

The county uses the ox fording a stream device of the City of Oxford. Formed at Bicester in May 1860 was the 7th Oxfordshire Rifle Volunteers Corps, the ox from the county this time getting its feet wet in the badge illustrated.

PADDINGTON (London)

Granted in 1902, the arms of this London borough display two wolves' heads and crossed swords passing through a mural crown. Paddington's first mayor was Sir John Aird, the heads coming from his arms, while the swords are a feature of those belonging to the See of London. Illustration from a 1930s official guide.

PADIHAM (Lancashire)

A quartered shield with a lamb in the first quarter in reference to the area's sheep farming. The town also employs many in its several engineering works and this is represented by an anvil in the second quarter. There is weaving too, and this has been symbolized in the third quarter which has a shuttle, the inclusion of this device serving a second purpose in as much as Lord Shuttleworth is an important landowner. The fourth and last quarter has a spray of red roses for Lancashire.

PENRYN (Cornwall)

The town seal shows the profile of a man's head wearing a laurel wreath. A C Scott-Giles mentions that he had been informed by the town clerk that the head was that of a Saracen. Could he, I wonder, be a representation of Peter Mundy (1600-1667), the famous merchant trader, traveller, writer and explorer who came from Penryn?

PENZANCE (Cornwall)

The seal includes the head of St John the Baptist on a plate together with the inscription 'Pensans anno

73

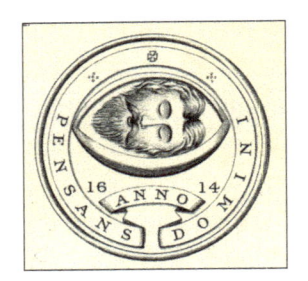

domini 1614', C W Scott-Gilles suggesting that the device was probably referring to the supposed derivation of the name Pen-san, 'Holy Head'. The date refers to the year that the town corporation adopted the seal.

PETERBOROUGH (Northamptonshire)

The gold keys of St Peter upon a blue shield. Also used is a shield divided red and blue, the red section being charged with gold keys and four gold crosses (these are the arms of the See of Peterborough), the blue having crossed swords and four crosses. The latter is a variation of the heraldry of the deanery.

PETERSFIELD (Hampshire)

A silver shield charged with a black ring between four roundels upon a red rose, all upon a silver shield, according to Burke's *General Armoury*.

PEVENSEY (Sussex)

Both the obverse and reverse of an ancient seal are described and illustrated in Gale Pedrick's *Borough Seals of the Gothic Period*. Pevensey was once a port of great importance and shows on its seal an ancient one-masted ship fully manned. Note the two men stationed on the sterncastle blowing trumpets. Gale Pedrick describes the half-figure below these as a knight. Still with the sea, the reverse of the seal shows two ships. There is a figure, mitred, with pastoral staff and with his right hand in benediction, which Gale Pedrick identifies as St Nicholas. The parish church at Pevensey is dedicated to St Nicholas.

PLYMOUTH (Devonshire)

A silver shield charged with a green cross and four black towers, the crest a gold coronet, the supporters two gold lions. A principal church in Plymouth is dedicated to St Andrew, the cross being thought to represent this. A C Fox-Davies tells of an older coat of arms recorded in the College of Arms which shows on a red shield a three-masted ship displaying the banner of St George. Plymouth, of course, was for centuries an important sea port and naval base.

PONTEFRACT (Yorkshire)

A silver castle on water upon a black ground, recorded by the Heralds in 1584. Pontefract Castle, where Richard II was imprisoned and supposedly starved to death in 1400, was built during the reign of William I by Ilbert de Lacy. The image shown in the 1893 edition of Debrett's *House of Commons* also includes the letter 'P', one each side of the castle's highest tower.

74

POOLE (Dorsetshire)

As an important seaport and with a strong connection to the sea, Poole's arms show water, shells, a dolphin and, as a crest, a mermaid holding an anchor. An ancient ship at sea also featureds on the town seal.

POPLAR (London)

The seal had three shields representing three of the borough's parishes: a gateway with a ship above for the inner dock gate of the West Indies Docks at All Saints, a bow-shaped bridge between two bows, for St Mary Stratford-le-Bow and the figure of a Benedictine monk in reference to Bromley-St Leonard. The bow-shaped bridge over the River Lea was built by Queen Matilda, wife of Henry I in 1100. Poplar was once an important centre of shipbuilding and the ship above the West India Dock's gateway recalls this.

PORTSMOUTH (Hampshire)

On a blue ground, a gold star above a gold crescent. A town much dependant on ships and the sea, the two symbols fit the Portsmouth motto, 'Heaven's light our guide'. An important naval base for centuries, the town is referred to as the 'Home of the Royal Navy'.

PRESTON (Lancashire)

On a blue shield, a silver Holy Lamb and the letters 'PP' in gold. The Holy Lamb is the emblem of St John the Baptist to whom Preston's parish church is dedicated. The town by the eighteenth century had gained a reputation of being a fashionable society centre and it is thought that the 'PP' letters were there to suggest a Proud Preston.

PRESTWICH (Lancashire)

The town seal has a representation of a mermaid with a comb in her left hand and a mirror in her right. The device is from the arms of the Prestwich family who held the manor at one time.

PUDSEY (Yorkshire)

On a green chevron, three gold spur-rowels with above, two pairs of crossed shuttles and below, a woolpack. The shuttles and woolpack represent local industries, the chevron and spur-rowels being from the arms of the Pudsey family. There is a border of white roses representing Yorkshire. These were the arms granted in 1901.

QUEENSBOROUGH (Kent)

The seal has a castle with the torso of a crowned women appearing from the upper battlements. This market town on the Isle of Sheppey was once called King's Castle after the building there of a fortified structure by Edward III from a design by William of Wykeham. So enamoured was Edward with his wife Philippa that he later changed the name of the place to Queensborough.

RADCLIFFE (Lancashire)

In reference to Ederton, Baron Grey de Radcliffe, half of the urban district's shield shows a red lion rampant between three black arrow heads on a silver ground. The right half is divided into two, the top having a gold fleur-de-lys on gold, the lower a gold lion on red. Both devices are from the arms of Lancaster.

RAMSGATE (Kent)

Father and son John and John Jr Shaw were the principal architects of Ramsgate Harbour, its lighthouse at the end of the south breakwater being completed in 1842. The crest shows a representation of the building on its pierhead location and issuing from a naval crown. Ramsgate, during the Napoleonic wars, served as the chief embarkation point for troop movements to Europe. The shield of the arms granted on 23 July 1884 shows two emblems connected with the sea, a dolphin and a ship, together with the half-lion-half ship of the Cinque Ports and Kent's white horse. A safe harbour and successful seaside resort, Ramsgate's motto translates as 'Safety to the shipwrecked, health to the sick'.

RAWDON (Yorkshire)

The urban district council uses the arms of the Rawdon family: a black bar and three black arrowheads on a silver shield. The crest has an arrowhead pointing down into a mural crown and with a spray of laurel placed into its opening.

RAWTENSTALL (Lancashire)

The Forest of Rossendale once surrounded Rawtenstall and here in the arms granted in 1891 we see a representation of the squirrels that once, it is said, could move from one end of the vast woodland to the other without leaving the treetops. Before the deforestation in Henry VII's time, wolves terrorised the area, especially the part of the borough that bore the name of Wolfenden Booth. Here on the red bar running across the centre of the shield we see one of them placed between two bales of wool which remind us of Rawtenstall's mills and its cotton industry. Less menacing are the two cows grazing at the bottom of the shield, there to recall the town's importance as a cattle farm as early as 1324. The borough includes a former hamlet called Cowpe. The king's deer roamed the old forest, a red hand cut off at the wrist reminding all of the penalty should you hunt and kill one of them. 'He prospers who labours.'

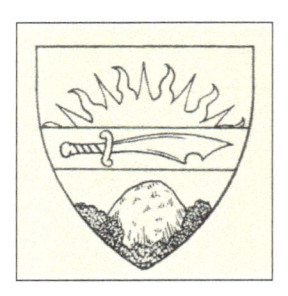

RAYLEIGH (Essex)

All that is left of the castle built just outside Rayleigh in the eleventh century are the earthwork remains of its motte-and-bailey. The sight is now known as Rayleigh Mount and a representation of it can be seen in the lower section of the urban district council's shield. Also seen is a seaxe from the arms of Essex, and the rays of the sun, presumably alluding to the name.

READING (Berkshire)

A blue shield charged with five gold heads couped at the neck were the arms recorded at the College of Arms after confirmation to the borough in 1566. The design was based on a thirteenth-century seal. Far from happy with the fact that her own son was not made king, Queen Æifthryth set plans afoot for the murder of her stepson, King of the English, Edward (975-978). But, sorry for her crime, in restitution she founded in Reading the Minster Church of St Mary the Virgin. It is though that the central crowned head is that of the assassinated Edward.

REDRUTH (Cornwall)

D Endean Ivall notes in his book *Cornish Heraldry and Symbolism* that a representation of Carn Brea Castle had long been used as the emblem of Redruth. The castle originated as a chapel in 1379 and is thought to have been dedicated to St Michael. A seal is also on record that shows a representation of a druid holding in one hand a sickle and in the other a spray of mistletoe. Behind him is a fire and an oak tree.

REIGATE (Surrey)

A C Fox-Davies illustrates the seal of the town in his 1894 edition of *The Book of Public Arms.* Here we see situated in front of a tree an embattled gateway with portcullis, below which are the letters 'REI' and the motto 'Never wonne ne never shall'. Placed within the branches of the tree is the gold and blue chequered shield of William de Warenne (2nd Earl of Surrey) who, in the twelfth century, held the manor and was responsible for the building of the castle around which the town grew.

RICHMOND (Surrey)

The town was once called Sheen and became Richmond after King Henry VII built his Richmond Palace about 1501. He was the Earl of Richmond in Yorkshire. The roses on their ermine ground, portcullises and lion on red are in reference to this royal association. The palace itself, which stands on the River Thames, is represented by the building in the centre of the shield. The Old Deer Park and Richmond Park are symbolised by the stag crest, the Thames by the swan. These arms were granted on 9 June 1891; the motto, 'For God and King'.

RICHMOND (Yorkshire)

The arms illustrated, with their orle and ermine diagonal band (a bend) were granted in 1665, C Wilfrid Scott-Giles noting that the former was possibly derived from the heraldry of Baliol of Barnard Castle. The Counts and Dukes of Brittany were associated with Richmond in the twelfth century, Brittany having just ermine in its arms. A C Fox-Davies in his *Book of Public Arms* quotes an item of interesting information that he had received from the town clerk. It concerns the common seal which, he notes, '…can be traced back as far as the earliest grants, it is the effigy of a venerable old man, with a long beard and a glory round his head, placed in a canopied shrine or tabernacle of Gothic structure, his cloak closed at the neck but thrown open before by his hands, which disclosed a crucifix hanging from his neck. On the dexter side of the tabernacle-work in which he is enshrined are the Arms of France and England quartered, and on the sinister side those of John I, Earl of Richmond.'

RIPON (Yorkshire)

On a red shield, a gold bugle with the letters 'R I P P O N' placed among the strings. Above this as a crest, a spur. A Wilfrid Scott-Giles in his *Civic Arms of*

77

England & Wales quotes from correspondence he had received from the town clerk. He notes that the bugle had featured in the arms of Ripon from time immemorial, 'but the spur [as a crest] was introduced at a more recent date, probably to signify the trade of spur-making from which the City was famous in the Middle Ages.' The town clerk goes on to explain the bugle which is the 'Charter Horn' carried by the Sergeant-at-Mace 'who precedes the Mayor with the Mace on all ceremonial occasions.' Rippon's charter as a borough was conferred in 886.

RISHTON (Lancashire)

The urban district council used a shield charged with a lion and the word *Reviresco*—'I grow green again'. The arms are based on those of the Rishton family.

ROCHDALE (Lancashire)

Here we have a fleece, woolpack and branches of a cotton tree representing Rochdale's textile industries. The production of woollen cloth, baize, kerseys and flannel were a main source of employment in the town since Henry VIII's time. And there is a millrind too remembering its iron works. A black border surrounds the central silver section of the shield upon which are set eight silver martlets. The birds are from the Rashdale and Dearden families, the latter coming into possession of the Manor of Rochdale in 1823. The arms were granted on 20 February 1857.

ROCHESTER (Kent)

A gold shield charged with a red cross bearing the letter 'R' in gold. Above this is the lion of England which recalls that Rochester was originally a Royal Borough. The illustrations are from an Edwardian postcard and the cap badge of the Rochester Volunteer Training Corps which was formed in 1914. Gale Pedrick in his detailed reference work *Borough Seals of the Gothic Period* illustrates both the obverse and reverse of an ancient seal used by the City of Rochester: a representation of Rochester Castle (obverse) and the martyrdom of St Andrew to whom Rochester Cathedral is dedicated.

ROMSEY (Hampshire)

The ancient town seal shows a portcullis in reference to Romsey Abbey which dates back to the tenth century.

ROTHERHAM (Yorkshire)

Industrialists Samuel and Aaron Walker began their Walker's Iron and Steel business in 1746, the Rotherham firm later proudly boasting that most of the guns used throughout the American War of Independence and Napoleonic wars were made at their several casting foundries. By 1781, notes one source, three-fifths of metal cast at the Walker's works was supplied to the government. Certainly, some eighty of the guns aboard HMS *Victory* were cast by the company and their mark 'W & Co' can be seen if you visit the ship at Portsmouth. 'Few people', notes the A Web of English History website, 'appear to know that Rotherham was once the main producer of cannon in the United Kingdom....They were made in large numbers by the Samuel Walker Company and up to 1,000 people were employed in their production. By 1795, they were making something like 22,000 cannon a year.' Arms were not officially granted to Rotherham until 22 October 1947, but the Corporation prior to this, however, had made use of the device illustrated. Much here, in the form of the three cannons and bridge in recognition of the employment the Walker brothers must have brought to the town. The latter is representing London's Southwark Bridge, for which 5,700 tons of ironwork was produced by Walker's. Here too are stag's heads from the arms of Thomas Rotherham (1423-1500), Archbishop of York and founder in the town of Jesus College, and representing commerce, Mercury's golden staff. 'Thus industry flourishes', reads the motto.

ROTHWELL (Northamptonshire)

Rothwell Urban District Council used a quartered shield representing several former holders of the manor: in the first two gold lions in reference to William the Conqueror, a red chevron for the Stafford family in the second and six green trefoils for the Treshams in the third. There is a pun here on the name, the trefoils resembling shamrocks. The fourth quarter represents two families, three black sleeves and a chevron for Maunsell, three blue cats for Tibbits. More puns: the sleeves are known heraldically as maunches (Maunsell) and the cats (Tibbits), domestic of course. The Treshams are also represented in the boar's head crest.

RUGBY (Warwickshire)

Chris J Smith in his booklet *The Civic Heraldry of Warwickshire* points out that when Rugby became an Urban District in 1894 it 'wrongfully' adopted the arms and crest of Lawrence Sheriff—three griffins' heads, a fleur-de-lys and two roses—together with the motto 'May Rugby flourish'. Lawrence Sheriff, who died in 1567, was from Brownsover just outside Rugby had become a wealthy grocer in London. He was the founder of Rugby School in 1567 who also used his arms.

RUTLAND

A horseshoe in reference to the custom at Oakham whereas every nobleman passing through the town for the first time has to present a horseshoe or a cash payment in lieu. The shoes are traditionally affixed to a wall at Oakham Castle.

RYDE (Isle of Wight)

On a silver ground a schooner yacht in full sail within a border of eight gold stars upon blue. These were the arms granted in February 1869 together with a crest made up of a seahorse charged with two gold stars on its body. C Wilfrid Scott-Giles gives the following, possible, explanation regarding the use of the stars, that they are in reference to the one in the arms of Portsmouth, which faces Ryde across Spithead. The popularity of Ryde as a seaside resort and centre of boating activities quickly grew after the merger of the villages of Upper and Lower Ryde in the eighteenth century.

RYE (Sussex)

The town uses the arms of the Cinque Ports, three demi lions joined to three rear ends of wooden ships. A town seal shows on the obverse a one-masted ship displaying flags charged with the cross of St George. St Mary, the patron saint of Rye, is featured on the reverse together with St Mary's Church, said to be the largest parish church in England.

ST ALBANS (Hertfordshire)

The ancient arms of St Albans Abbey display on a blue ground, a sword and crown upon a gold saltire cross. For the City of St Albans, the same without the sword and crown. The Edwardian postcard illustrated shows the city arms together with a photograph of the nave at St Albans Cathedral.

ST ANNES-ON-SEA (Lancashire)

The arms in use prior to 1922 and the link with Lytham consisted of a quartered shield showing a lighthouse, an ancient ship, a lion and a tower. The crest was an arm in armour holding a sword behind which were placed two golf clubs. C Wilfrid Scott-Giles makes the comment that this is the only case he has come across where golf clubs have been used in municipal insignia. They refer to the St Annes Golf Lincs which were founded in 1901 and long been considered as one of the finest in England. The crest is that of the Clifton family who did much towards the prosperity of St Annes and neighbouring Lytham. Illustrated is an Edwardian heraldic postcard which simply shows a view all-important to the town: the sea. Here is the pier which was opened to the public in 1885 and a representation of the Ribble lighthouse built in 1848.

ST ASAPH (Cornwall)

Two silver keys upon a black ground taken from the See of St Asaph. The Rev E E Dorling in his book *The Arts of the Church, Heraldry of the Church* points out that 'There is no obvious reason for the reference of the keys to this saint or to the see that bears his name.'

ST HELENS (Lancashire)

Granted in 1876, the St Helens arms were based on those of local families. Here we have blue bars for Parr, a black cross and fleur-de-lis for Eccleston, red saltire crosses for Gerard, griffins for Bold, a lion for Walmsley and another fleur-de-lis for Sir David Gamble who was the first mayor and benefactor of the town. 'Light out of the earth' translates the motto which is in reference to the town's contribution to light via its coal resources.

ST IVES (Cornwall)

In reference to the name of the town, St Ives uses a silver shield completely covered with green ivy.

ST IVES (Huntingdonshire)

Equally well known for its chapel on a bridge and as a centre for trade and navigation, the Borough of St Ives when it was incorporated as such in 1874 chose as its arms the heads of four bulls in reference to the town's centuries-old wide reputation for markets. 'By toil, not by sleep' translates the motto. A C Fox-Davies, who preferred his heraldry designs adhering strictly to the rules, was far from happy with the artist's work and writes of 'a lamentable ignorance of heraldry on somebody's part. The bull's heads,' he points out, 'are far from heraldic, being neither couped, erased, nor cabossed… They have a remarkable resemblance to Messrs Colman's trade-mark.' And then the ultimate condemnation, 'Had the original artist no better copy to guide him than an old mustard-tin?'

ST MARYLEBONE (London)

In the crest we have St Mary and in the lower part of the shield wavy lines representing an old stream (or bourne) called Tybourne (or Tyburn). An ancient chapel dedicated to St Mary was founded on the banks of Tyburn by Barking Abbey. From the abbey's heraldry comes the rose and lilies, the fleur-de-lis that of the local Portman family. 'Let it be done according to Thy Word' translates the motto. St Marylebone's arms were granted in 1901.

ST MAWES (Cornwall)

The blue shield is divided by a gold line of lozenges, the top half showing a tower, the lower a ship of three masts. St Mawes Castle dates from the time of Henry VIII, the town being close to the sea and once well known for its fishing industry.

ST PANCRAS (London)

The arms adopted by the borough in 1901 show in its centre a representation of St Pancras, the young Phrygian noble previously featuring on a council seal. He is depicted with book in hand while trampling his enemies underfoot. In the first quarter of the shield we see a gold cross on a blue ground, the second and third being taken from the arms of Lewes near Brighton. Lewes was the first town in England to consecrate a church to the memory of St Pancras. The borough formed part of the County of Middlesex, the arms of which can be seen in the remaining quarter. A sun was used as a crest to symbolize the dawn of Christianity in the borough.

SAFFRON WALDEN (Essex)

W Gurney Benham shows a sketch in his 1916 book, *Borough & Council Arms of Essex,* of the earliest known seal of Saffron Walden. Dating from the time of

Edward IV, the seal bears a crowned lion and the fleur-de-lis of France which are both royal emblems. A charter of incorporation was granted in 1549 and with it a seal bearing a coat of arms based on a punning reference to the name of the town: three saffron flowers within a wall.

SALFORD (Lancashire)

Here we have bees representing industry, shuttles and a cotton bale for Salford's textile mills and millrinds for its production of iron. There is a wolf and wheatsheaves in reference to the fact that Salford was at one time part of the Earldom of Chester before it passed to the Earls of Lancaster and became part of the Duchy which had an antelope in its heraldry. The arms and supporters were granted in 1844.

SALISBURY (Wiltshire)

A shield charged with four gold and four blue bars, between two gold two-headed eagles with blue coronets about their necks as supporters. These arms were recorded by the Heralds in 1565. C Wilfrid Scott-Giles in his research for Salisbury's arms, notes information that he received from the Salisbury, South Wilts and Blackmore Museum. The Controller makes the point that there are several theories regarding the origins of Salisbury's arms. He mentions the suggestion that the blue bars represent the four rivers which meet in the city, and that the eagles are from the arms of the Bouverie family who were great benefactors of the city. But, as he rightly points out, the Bouveries were still Huguenot refugees in Canterbury when the grant was made, and yet to be known in Salisbury.

SALTASH (Cornwall)

Two seals have been recorded for Saltash where Isambard Kingdom Brunel's Royal Albert Bridge was opened by HRH Prince Albert on 2 May 1859. The first shows a three-masted ship at anchor, while the other uses the arms of the ancient Earls of Cornwall, Lords of Saltash: namely silver with a red lion rampant within a black border charged with eight bezants. On either side are ostrich feathers, the emblems of the Prince of Wales, Duke of Cornwall, and above a prince's coronet made up of crosses and fleur-de-lis. The shield and feathers have been placed upon water.

SANDWICH (Kent)

Once a major port and one of the Cinque Ports, Sandwich is now some three miles from the sea, its arms having three half-lions joined to the hulks of three silver ship's. The town, which saw the import of the first captive elephant in Britain by the emperor Claudius, also used a seal which featured on its obverse a one-masted ship at sea. Two of her crew are sitting on the yard furling the mainsail while in the hold can be seen two soldiers, one holding an axe and the other a flag charged with a star. A pilot holding a boat hook occupies the stern of the vessel. The reverse of the seal comprises a lion of England between two trees.

82

SCARBOROUGH (Yorkshire)

There was once an Iron Age settlement here; the Romans had a signal station on the same site and the Anglo-Saxons later built a chapel there. William le Gros, the powerful Anglo-Norman baron, put a wooden castle in its place, then about 1157 along came Henry II who decided stone would be better. Scarborough Castle, overlooking the town and the North Sea, is represented in the borough's ancient seal. An important harbour, here too is a ship with a crew of two and a star to guide them.

SEAFORD (Sussex)

Once, in the Middle Ages, Seaford could lay claim to being one of the main ports serving the south of England, but constant raids by French pirates and the eventual silting up of its harbour would put a stop to that. The people of the town later took to the looting of ships wrecked in the bay and when there were none to plunder, could it be true that they produced their own by putting fake harbour lights on the cliffs? But good or bad it earnt the townspeople the nickname 'cormorants' or 'shags'. The design taken from an ancient seal, here in the arms illustrated on this Edwardian postcard we see a ship in reference to the port, and a bird recalling the nickname.

SELBY (Yorkshire)

Selby Urban District Council had a shield charged with three silver swans, the arms of Selby Abbey which was founded in 1069.

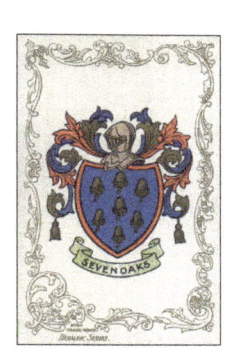

SEVENOAKS (Kent)

For the Sevenoaks Urban District Council, what else but seven acorns. The original seven oak trees in Knole Pork have been replaced several times.

SHAFTESBURY (Dorsetshire)

In 880 Alfred the Great founded a fortified settlement here to hinder Danish invaders. He built Shaftesbury Abbey eight years later and established two royal mints which struck coins bearing the name of the town. The relics of St Edward the Martyr were received at the abbey in 981, King Canute died in Shaftesbury and Edward the Confessor set up a third mint. When the Domesday Book was compiled, ownership of the town was firmly in the hands of the king and the abbey. In use by 1570 were the arms illustrated, the quarters and cross being silver and blue, the fleur-de-lis blue, leopards, silver. The charges certainly suggest a royal connection.

SHEFFIELD (Yorkshire)

Think of Sheffield and you think of steel. Think of Sheffield steel and into your mind come knives, forks and spoons. Stainless steel and crucible steel were developed in Sheffield which boosted its cutlery trade and with it, its population, by more than ten times. With such tremendous industry in the area the town would be elevated to a city in 1893 and with this distinction came the addition of supporters to its arms: the mighty Thor with his hammer and Vulcan, the god of fire, complete with anvil and pincers. Long in use, the original arms displayed a collection of eight arrows to illustrate Sheffield's piercing trade. The lion crest represents holders of the manor, the Earls of Shrewsbury, the golden wheatsheaves on a green ground the name of the city which stands on the River Sheaf. 'By God's help labour succeeds' translates the motto. The 1874 edition of Debrett's *House of Commons* shows the seal of the mayor, aldermen and burgesses of the Borough of Sheffield which also includes the figure of an angel.

SHILDON (Durham)

Three shields between two picks and a hammer representing the town's achievements in mining and engineering. Shildon also owes much of its prosperity to the railway and it was here that Timothy Hackworth built his famous locomotive *Royal George* in 1827. The first shield shows a representation of the engine on a red ground. The second referes to the local family of Byerley who resided at Middridge Grange, the third is for the Lilburns of East Thickley.

SHIPLEY (Yorkshire)

Shipley Urban District Council used the device of a sheep in a field, the background showing a windmill and trees. As the name of the town suggests (roughly a forest clearing used for sheep), Shipley has long been associated with sheep grazing and the production of wool textiles. The River Aire would provide a ready source of water to power the many mills.

SHOREDITCH (London)

John de Northampton was Lord Mayor of London in 1381-82 and his controversial policies earnt him the alternative name of John Comberton, chroniclers playing on the word for trouble which was 'comber'. Ousted in the 1383 election, he was then charged with sedition on 7 February 1384 and subsequently sentenced to ten years imprisonment, after which he returned to London where he died in 1397. But, like him or loathe him, it would be his arms, two lions sharing one head, that were chosen as those for Shoreditch. The motto, 'More light, more power', was added in reference to the Shoreditch Electricity Generating Station and Refuse Destructor at Cornet Street in 1897.

SHOREHAM (Sussex)

The Norman conquerors did much to advance the place, the writer Muhammad al-Idrisi recording in about 1153 that Shoreham was 'a fine and cultivated city containing buildings and flourishing activity.' And with the arrival of the railway in 1840, Shoreham quickly prospered as a port. The De Braose family held the manor and it would be on their arms that those of Shoreham were based—a blue lion among black crosses. The three lions on the right side of the shield are those of England.

SHREWSBURY (Shropshire)

Just nine miles from the Welsh border, Shrewsbury was once the scene of numerous conflicts between the Welsh and English. Here too took place, just to the north of the town, the Battle of Shrewsbury between King Henry IV and Henry Hotspur Percy. The former would emerge victorious, as we can hear about in Shakespeare's Henry IV, Part 1, Act 5. There is no exact date available for the introduction of Shrewsbury's arms, but they were certainly part of the town seal of 1425 and can be seen in the Market Hall which was built in 1595. Three gold leopards' faces, locally referred to as 'loggerheads', on a blue ground and the motto *'Floreat Salopia'*.

SHROPSHIRE

The seal of Shropshire County Council is beautiful engraved with the shields belonging to six Shropshire towns: Shrewsbury, Bridgnorth, Ludlow, Oswestry, Wenlock and Bishop's Castle. The three leopards' faces (or loggerheads) from the arms of the county town of Shrewsbury are used by Shropshire too. They were granted in 1896 and can be seen on three blue piles on a ground of gold with black ermine spots.

SIDCUP (Kent)

Sidcup Urban District Council used the white horse and motto *'Invicta'* from the arms of Kent.

SITTINGBOURNE AND MILTON (Kent)

The urban district council used the device of a wyvern.

SMETHWICK (Staffordshire)

Here in this Wills cigarette card representation of the borough seal we see local industry and achievement in the form of machinery, a lighthouse, a gas works and a smith busily at work at his anvil. In the town the iron and steel industry employed many, the gas works recalling the part William Murdoch played in the introduction of gas lighting. When arms were granted on 15 November 1907 other symbols were used and here instead we see a flaming beacon for gas and the emblem of the Planet Mars for the iron and steel. The caduceus of Mercury was also included which symbolizes commerce, and to go with this the motto *'Labore et Ingenio'* (By industry and ingenuity). From the arms of James Watt we have a wooden club, those of Sir James Timmins Chance, a demi-lion crest and from Matthew Boulton the arrow it holds. Brought into service in May 1779 was the Smethwick Engine manufactured by Boulton and Watt which pumped water up to the 491 foot summit level of the old Birmingham Canal at Smethwick. Employed by Boulton and Watt was William Murdoch, the Scottish engineer to whom we must thank for gas lighting. Sir James Timmins Chance was an English industrialist and was thought of as an expert on lighthouse optics. He was the grandson of William Chance, the founder of the family firm of Chance Brothers Glassworks in Smethwick.

SOMERSETSHIRE

Without its own arms, the county sometimes used those belonging to Bath. Arms were, however, granted in 1911 and these comprised a red dragon holding a blue mace on a gold ground. C Wilfrid Scott-Giles points out that the dragon is that of the ancient Kingdom of the West Saxons.

SOUTH MOLTON (Devonshire)

It was at South Molton on 14 March 1655 that Sir John Penruddock was taken prisoner after a lengthy street fight with troops of the New Model Army under the command of Captain Unton Cook. And so, it is said, came to an end the plans devised by Penruddock and the organisation known as 'The Sealed Knot' to put Charles II back on the throne of England. South Moulton has been described as a well-built market town trading mostly in sheep and here we see one of them as part of the town's shield. Also seen is a bishop's mitre (the village of Bishop's Nympton is just three miles to the east of South Moulton) and a crown.

SOUTH SHIELDS (Durham)

He began as an apprentice to a house painter then moved on to become the parish clerk at South Shields. William Wouldhave (1751-1821) recognised, along with Lionel Lukin, as the inventor of the lifeboat. Shortly after the disaster that saw the passengers and crew of the *Adventure* drowned near the coast at the mouth of the River Tyne, a competition was set up to design a boat for saving lives at sea. With a cork lining, Wouldhave's boat was to be self-righting if it should overturn in a heavy sea and was to be built in 1789 by South Shields boatbuilder Henry Greathead. Turning now to the arms of South Shields, C Wilfrid Scott-Giles refers to information received from the town clerk who states that the design was that of South Shields artist Robinson Elliott. Here then is a representation of the town's lifeboat and crew and supporters symbolising courage (in the sailor) and commerce by the female figure who holds a caduceus, the staff of Hermes, god of commerce. The two words, along with Humanity which is represented by the lifeboat, can be seen in the motto.

SOUTHAM (Warwickshire)

The common seal in use prior to a grant of arms in 1959 originally bore a crown within a border inscribed 'Southam Rural District Council'. But the crown was later removed, leaving the space inside the border blank.

SOUTHAMPTON (Hampshire)

From its arms there can be no doubt that this county borough has a strong connection with the sea. Here in the midst of waves are two ships, both of them flying the pennon of St George. Two gold lions standing on the bowls of ships guard the shield which has roses representing both York and Lancaster. Justice too is here in the form of the crest. These were the arms granted in 1575. Southampton had become a major port for travel between Winchester, then capital of England, and Normandy following the Norman Conquest of 1066. It was at Southampton that Henry V collected his army prior to sailing for France and the eventual Battle of Agincourt. Southampton Castle was built during the twelfth century. Shipbuilding had become an important industry during the Middle Ages, Henry V's well-known warship, HMS *Grace Dieu,* being launched there in 1418. Also illustrated is a seventeenth-century seal showing a single ship and the arms of three roses as shown in Debrett's *House of Commons*.

SOUTHEND-ON-SEA (Essex)

Prior to the granting of arms on 1 January 1915, this well-known Essex seaside resort used a device that included a well, a church and the resort's most popular attraction, its more than a mile long pier. Recalling close by districts, the authorized arms used none of these and instead we see the anchor of St Clement, the patron saint of Leigh, of whom legend has it that he was bound to an anchor and thrown into the sea, the gridiron of Eastwood's St Lawrence, the Holy Trinity trefoil symbol from Southchurch and, from the old seal of St Mary's Priory at Prittlewell, a vase of lilies. At Prittlewell, its 'South End' now better known, there was a Cluniac foundation and one of its monks now forms the right supporter. He is accompanied on the other side by a medieval fisherman holding a net who represents a longstanding industry in Southend. For a crest and reminding us of the place's connection with the sea, a ship's mast complete with crow's nest flies the banner of St George. *'Per mare per ecclesiam'*; strong indeed is Southend's connection with both church and sea. Formed for service during the 1st World War was the Southend Battalion Volunteer National Guard, and its cap badge using the arms is also shown.

SOUTHPORT (Lancashire)

William Sutton, locally called 'The Mad Duke', enjoyed frequent evenings of entertainment in his Black Bull Inn where he delighted all with his violin playing. He also liked sea bathing and, thinking that this would be a good way to add to his income, in 1792 built a bathing house in the sparsely populated South Hawes. This then was the beginning of Southport and the start of one of Lancashire's most popular seaside resorts. Unofficial arms were later drawn up by Doctor Craven, a local councillor who, it is said, seems to have based the design on those of his own. The central bar and crosses are his. In Southport's Duke Street Cemetery there is a memorial to the crew of the town's lifeboat who lost their lives on the night of 9 December 1886 as they made desperate efforts to save the men of the cargo ship *Mexico*, then in difficulty off Southport. The entire crew of the St Anne's boat were lost, making a total with those from Southport of twenty-eight. This would be the worst lifeboat disaster in the history of Britain. Interestingly, when Southport's arms were officially granted in 1923, they were more or less identical to Doctor Craven's design, save for the fact that the lifeboat had been replaced by a sailing ship. Two years later the RNLI closed their station at Southport.

SOUTHWARK (London)

Located on the south side of the River Thames, Southwark was, until 1889, part of Surrey. The name means 'southern fortifications' and originates from the time of the Danish invasion. There soon developed an important trading place, the Borough Market still operating today as it always had, in the shadow of Southwark Cathedral. Here too was Shakespeare's Globe Theatre and several prisons, the 'Clink' included.

Prior to the granting of arms to the borough on 14 June 1902, the circle and cross device seen in the first illustration were in use. This was referred to as the 'Southwark Cross' and was taken from the mark of the Bridge House Estates Committee of the City of London seen on their bridges and buildings. See it still on Tower Bridge. The arms introduced in 1902 consisted of a quartered shield, the Southwark Cross being retained in the third quarter as a representative of the parish of St George the Martyr. The remaining quarters also represent Southwark's parishes: a rose for St Mary Overie (the cathedral is dedicated to St Saviour and St Overie), the white lily of St Mary Newington and a stag's head in red which comes from the arms of the parish of Christ Church.

SOUTHWOLD (Suffolk)

A small town on the North Sea coast, Southwold was almost completely destroyed by a fire in 1659, St Edmund's Church being badly damaged. Here too, in 1672, took place the Battle of Sole Bay between the English and a combined fleet of French and Dutch ships. The dedication of the parish church explains the gold crown and crossed arrows that form the main charge of the black shield. These are from the insignia of St Edmund, King and Martyr who can be seen as the crest. Not seen in the A C Fox-Davies illustration shown is the town motto 'They right defend'.

SOWERBY (Yorkshire)

The shield used by Sowerby Urban District Council displayed a tower and a landscape including a bridge. Above the shield, a fleece. A Norman castle once stood at the high end of the town, the bridge representing that which crosses the River Calder upon which the town stands.

STAFFORD (Staffordshire)

Here on the red shield of Stafford we see the Stafford Knot, for the origins of which there are several explanations. Most popular is the story of a hangman who was faced with the dilemma of having to execute three criminals on the same day. But he only had one rope, and rather than give precedence over the other two by selecting one man first, he formed his rope in such a way that there were three loops, sufficient to put to death all three at the same time. Linked with this tale is another theory that at one time Stafford was so infested with thieves and murderers that it became necessary to hang them three at a time. Alternatively, if we bring to mind that when Staffordshire received its arms in January 1931, included was the motto 'The knot unites'. This then could link up with a third explanation as to the origins of the Stafford Knot. There had been trouble between Stafford and two other nearby areas, and it is told that, to put an end to this conflict Ethelfleda, the eldest daughter of Alfred the Great, symbolically took off her girdle and said to the local lords 'With this girdle, I bind us all as one.' The three areas subsequently became Staffordshire. Here too in the arms is a castle, Stafford having two, one the property of the king, the other that owned by the Earls of Stafford, and the lion of England. Debrett's *House of Commons* includes a fish below the castle in its illustration.

STAFFORDSHIRE

Prior to arms being granted in January 1931, the county council used a seal made up of a red chevron charged with the Stafford Knot, surrounded by a cord twisted into four similar knots. Between the knots were representations of local industries: a wheatsheaf for agriculture, a black lozenge for the coal fields, a ewer for pottery and the astronomical symbol of the Planet Mars for iron.

STALYBRIDGE (Cheshire)

The arms granted on 18 June 1857 recall several important families of the area. From the Staveleys, who held the manor and from whom the name of the town originates, we have the silver and red chevron of the shield. The crosses represent the Dukinfield family, the star (a spur-rowel) is that of the Asshetons and the cinquefoils, those from the heraldry of Astley. The wolf and wheatsheaf are in reference to the Earldom of Chester.

STAMFORD (Lincolnshire)

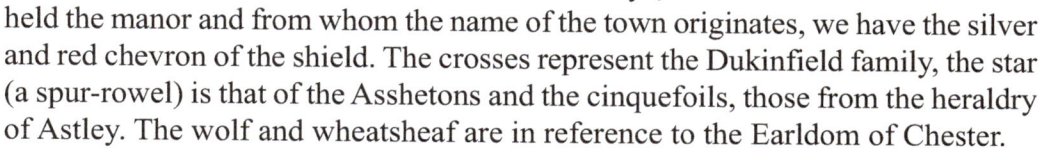

The Romans were there, the Anglo-Saxons chose it as their main town and later faced the Danes across the River Welland on which Stamford stands. A Norman castle was built there in about 1075, and Stamford Fair, as mentioned in Shakespeare's *Henry IV,* would become the largest in Lincolnshire. And do not forget that once Stamford was regarded as an important seat of learning, its colleges in the thirteenth century threatening to supersede even Oxford. But none of this history reached the arms of the town. Instead we have the gold and blue chequers of the Earls of Warenne, who held the manor in the thirteenth century, and the three lions of England. There is a thought that the latter were awarded as a thank-you to the men of Stafford who fought in the Battle of Loosecoat Field in 1469. St Mary is the chief patron of Stamford and a fourteenth-century seal exists showing her seated within a canopy supported by two pinnacle towers.

STEPNEY (London)

Arms were not granted to this London borough until 1931, but the design of the common seal in use prior to that illustrated figures representing the patron saints associated with Stepney's principal parish churches: St Anne's at Limehouse, St Mary Matfelon at Whitechapel, Stepney's St Dunstan's and St George's in the East. In the centre is the White Tower of the Tower of London which also forms part of the borough. There is a ship at the bottom of the seal, there to represent St Katherine's and adjoining docks, to the left a railway train in memory of the old Stepney and Blackwall Railway Company and on the right a loom symbolising the onetime important industry in the area, silk weaving. There is a second ship, at the top this time, which, according to Richard Crosley in his *London's Coats of Arms and the Stories They Tell,* '…was formerly used by the authorities of the ecclesiastical parish of Stepney to perpetrate the old tradition that any person born on the high seas was entitled to claim Stepney as his or her birthplace.' There is of course the old rhyme, 'He who sails on the wide sea/Is a parishioner of Stepney'. Indeed, St Dunstan's Church welcomed registration of children born at sea. It was known as the Church of the High Seas, due to its high congregation of sailors, and the Red Ensign of the Merchant Navy could often be seen flying from the tower.

STOCKBRIDGE (Hampshire)

The bridge that once crossed the River Test was made out of stocks, an old name for tree trunks. Stockbridge crosses the river and it was here that Edward I stayed in August 1294 and James II on his way to meet up with the armies of the Prince of Orange in November 1688. He dined, apparently, at the Swan Inn which still survives. Richard I granted a market there, Henry III extending it to a three-day event. The town grew and prospered, but tragedy later came in the form of a plague, causing the market confirmed by both Henry V and Henry VI to be closed down. Certainly the town has a close connection with royalty, its arms resembling those of England—three red lions on a gold ground.

STOCKPORT (Cheshire)

A C Fox-Davies records in 1915 that Stockport has no armorial bearings of its own but instead used those which appear to have belonged to 'the ancient family of Stopford, Stopfort, or Stockport, Barons of Stockport.' He describes a shield of gold lozenges and crosses on a blue ground. He also mentions how *Debrett's House of Commons* adds a description of supporters in the form of a lion, appearing from behind the shield, while to the right stands the figure of Britannia. This is the version used by W D & HO Wills in their 1905 'Borough Arms' set of cigarette cards. A scroll has been added which refers to the 1836 Corporate Reform Act.

STOCKTON-ON-TEES (Durham)

Shipbuilding in Stockton began in the fifteenth century, its port rapidly expanding in trade as engineering became an important industry. It was here that George Stephenson's Stockport to Darlington Railway began, which changed the world forever. Surprisingly, no reference to the railway appears in the town's arms. But we do have an anchor representing the docks and ships. The castle is that of the Norman Prince Bishops of Durham which dates from the twelfth century. It began life as a hall occupied by Bishop Hugh Pudsey and was first referred to as a castle in 1376.

STOKE NEWINGTON (London)

No official grant of arms are in possession of the Borough of Stoke Newington, records Richard Crosley in 1928, which had been formed by the amalgamation of Stoke Newington in London, and the urban district of South Horsey, Middlesex. But the council did adopt a design in 1900 which showed in the upper section of the shield a representation of the old parish church of St Mary. This church would become too small for the congregation, so the well-known designer George Gilbert Scott was commissioned to build a new one. It was consecrated in 1858 and now stands side-by-side with the old church. The lower part of the shield is divided into three, one being charged with the arms of the City of London, a second has the portcullis of Westminster, the third the three seaxes of Middlesex. Richard Crosley mentions that the name Stoke Newington denotes 'the new town or village by or in the wood', the place once being part of the great forest of Middlesex; this is reflected by the inclusion of a tree as a crest.

STOKE-ON-TRENT (Staffordshire)

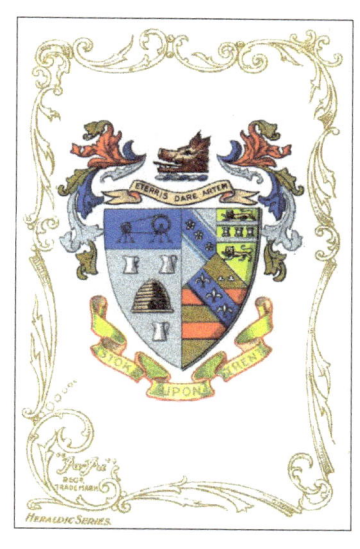

In A C Fox-Davies's 1894 edition of *The Book of Public Arms,* he mentions that Stoke had no armorial bearings and having had no help from the town clerk regarding his request for a copy of the town seal, resorted to the '…achievement upon the stationery for particulars of the Arms in use.' He describes the complex shield as having a 'beehive' (he adds to this comment that it could be a pottery kiln) between three jugs and representations of certain 'complicated machinery'. All this on the left side of the shield, the right having three cinquefoils, three ermine spots between two lions, three boars' heads and another serving as a crest. These are, in fact, the arms depicted in 1905 by WD & HO Wills as part of their 'Borough Arms' cigarette card set and an heraldic postcard by Ja-Ja of the same year. Arms were, however, granted on 20 March 1912 following the merger into one borough of Stoke-on-Trent, Burslem, Fenton, Hanley, Longton and Tunstall, and a drawing of these appeared in A C Fox-Davies's 1915 edition. Items from the arms of the several towns were used in the new design, the representation of an Egyptian potter being a welcome addition and joining several of the other charges in recognition of the area's well-known potteries.

STOURBRIDGE (Worcestershire)

The arms granted on 6 November 1917 show a bridge and two pears and in doing so reflect the name of the town, which stands on the Rive Stour, and its county. A pear tree is a feature of the arms of Worcestershire County Council. Important to the town was its woollen industry, which is represented by the fleece, and the manufacture of chains. It has also been suggested that brickwork was chosen to illustrate the bridge as a symbol of the town's many brickworks.

STRATFORD-UPON-AVON (Warwickshire)

When A C Fox-Davies was preparing both his 1894 and 1915 volumes of *The Book of Public Arms* he was able to illustrate the arms recorded in the College of Arms but provide no detail of the colours used. C Wilfrid Scott-Giles in 1933, on the other hand, gives a blue chevron on a gold ground. The leopards' faces are in natural colours. Chris J Smith, in his booklet *The Civic Heraldry of Warwickshire* notes that the earliest common or great seal of the borough is contemporary with Stratford's first charter from John de Coutances, Bishop of Worcester, which was dated 1196. The seal shows a chevron between three leopards' faces. Mr Smith points out that the origin of the arms is unknown, having no connection with any local family. It would be difficult to think of Stratford-upon-Avon without thinking of William Shakespeare and his wife Ann Hathaway whom he loved so much that in his will left her his 'second best bed'. The postcard illustrated, showing Ann's cottage together with the Stratford-upon-Avon arms, was posted in 1919.

SUDBURY (Suffolk)

Once popular among the gentry for its hunting skills, the now extinct Talbot was a breed of white dog said to have originated in Normandy. Here in the Sudbury arms granted in 1576 we see two of them, one on a black ground, the other serving between two feathers as a crest. The use of this device is in reference to an early benefactor of the town, one Simon of Sudbury who had upset the population by introducing poll tax. Having entered the Tower of London for safety, on 14 June 1381 its doors were opened to an angry mob who dragged him to Tower Hill where they removed his head. His body can be found buried in Canterbury Cathedral, but his skull found its way back to Sudbury and St Peter's Church. The Talbot is from his heraldry, the use of the lion and fleur-de-lis on a red ground is said to represent a royal connection with the town. Certainly it was Edward III who was responsible for settling the Flemings in the area, the family that went on to bring prosperity to Sudbury during the Middle Ages through weaving and silk.

SUFFOLK

A C Fox-Davies in both his volumes of *The Book of Public Arms* (1894, 1915) points out that Suffolk has no armorial bearings and that those of Ipswich are frequently used. But he goes on to say that both the councils of East and West Suffolk have seals. The 1894 edition illustrates both: West Suffolk has the arms of King Edward the Confessor, East, a representation of a castle with a lion above.

SUNDERLAND (Durham)

According to Arthur Charles Fox-Davies in his 1894 *The Book of Public Arms,* Sunderland had no official arms. The author, however, does mention that Debrett's *House of Commons* recalls an intended heraldic achievement design for the town, namely a sextant. Also mentioned is a terrestrial globe as a crest, and the motto '*Nil Desperandum Auspice Deo*' (With God as our leader there is no cause for despair). The two devices have been apt for Sunderland and its shipbuilding and maritime activities on the River Wear since the fourteenth century. The motto is taken from that leading Roman lyric poet, Horace. The 3rd Durham Rifle Volunteer Corps was formed at Sunderland on 6 March 1860 and included six companies by 1862 with Major Lord Adolphus Vane Tempest in command. Much of the corps was recruited from shipbuilding workers, the coal trade and those employed in the manufacture of anchors and chain cable. Illustrated is the sextant and globe devices as seen on a 1905 postcard and how they were used on a pouch-belt plate worn by the 3rd Durham Rifle Volunteers.

SURBITON (Surrey)

At the top of St Mark's Hill is one of Surbiton's two parish churches, the urban district council showing on its seal the winged lion emblematic of the AD 68 martyr. The Edwardian Ja-Ja postcard illustrated also shows a ship with the St Mark's lion on its sail.

SURREY

The seal of Surrey County Council had three shields within a trefoil shape: that for Warrens, Earls of Surrey, Kingston-upon-Thames and Guildford. Lions from the Royal Arms were placed within the gaps formed by the trefoil which ended with fleur-de-lis inside. The latter are from the arms of Mr Leycester Penrhyn who was the first Chairman of the County Council of Surrey. County councils were first introduce in 1889.

SUSSEX

For Sussex we have two coats of arms, that for the County Council of West Sussex with its six gold martlets, and the East Sussex County Council which displayed a quartered shield. Both were granted in 1889. The martlets date from medieval times when the Heralds assigned them to the ancient Kingdom of the South Saxons. Martlets are included in the quartered shields of East Sussex, the others representing the Warennes who held the Manor of Lewes (2nd quarter), Prevensey (third quarter) and the Cinque Ports (fourth quarter).

SUTTON COLDFIELD (Warwickshire)

Thanks to the efforts of Bishop John Vesey, King Henry VIII in 1528 declared that in future Sutton Coldfield should be known as Royal Sutton Coldfield. The use of a double heraldic rose on the town seal was most likely to recall the event. It would not be until May 1935 when arms were granted that the good bishop was recognised, along with the Tudors.

SUTTON-IN-ASHFIELD (Nottinghamshire)

From the arms of the Snitterton family, a silver snipe with a gold crown around its neck on a red ground. C Wilfrid Scott-Giles points out that the urban district council seems to have taken into use the snipe under the misapprehension that it appertained to the local family of Sutton, one of whom married a Snitterton.

SWAFFHAM (Norfolk)

The urban district council had a shield charged with two crossed keys and two crossed swords in reference to the Church of St Peter and St Paul. Built on the site of an original church, the present St Peter and St Paul's dates from 1454.

SWANAGE (Dorsetshire)

As a pun on its name, Swanage Urban District Council used the device of a swan in its arms.

SWINDON (Wiltshire)

Here in the arms granted to Swindon in 1901 we recall three notable people associated with the town. The three red crescents are those of the Goddard family who held the Manor of Swindon from 1560. Much of New Swindon was built on land belonging to the Vilett family and it is their three silver castles that appear in the second quarter of the shield. In the third quarter is the mitre belonging to Odo, Bishop of Bayeux in Normandy. After the Norman Conquest the Manor of Swindon was made a present of to

Odo by his half-brother William the Conqueror. Isambard Kingdom Brunel's Great Western Railway was well under way when Swindon was selected as a place to set up premises for the manufacture, repair and maintenance of its locomotives. By the middle of the twentieth century the GWR's works were Swindon's largest employer providing jobs for more than 14,500 workers. Much relating to the railway can be seen in the arms. Here in the upper part of the shield is the '4-2-2' engine *Lord of the Isle* which was designed by Daniel Gooch and exhibited at the 1851 Great Exhibition in London. The winged wheel is there to symbolise the swiftness and motion of railway travel, the hammers in the crest to denote the industry that was so important to Swindon and are depicted in gold to typify prosperity.

TAMWORTH (Staffordshire)

Queen Elizabeth I granted Tamworth a charter in 1560 and it is thought that the beautifully decorated fleur-de-lis of the town's seventeenth-century seal recalls this.

TAUNTON (Somersetshire)

It was here that a great Cornish army led by Perkin Warbeck during the Second Cornish uprising of 1497 surrendered to Henry VII. Then on 20 June 1685, and during the Monmouth Rebellion, the Duke of Monmouth crowned himself King of England. And then came the 'Bloody Assizes', the trials conducted by Judge Jeffreys, which took place in Taunton's castle. But it is the priory founded in Henry I's time by William Giffard, Bishop of Winchester, that is represented by the crown and cherub seen in the first illustration. The design being based on a seal of dated 1685. The motto. 'Let us defend' is in reference to the several civil war sieges of 1644-45 in which Taunton stood fast and refused to surrender to Royalist forces. Another seal exists and is illustrated by A C Fox-Davies in the 1894 edition of his book *The Book of Public Arms*. Here we see two peacocks (one would be used as a crest in the arms granted in October 1934) a fleur-de-lis, and a representation of, according to Fox-Davies, 'a castle or abbey', the croziers and cross, it is thought, possibly suggesting the latter.

TAVISTOCK (Devonshire)

The royal emblems, the lion and fleur-de-lis, are most probably there in recognition of the fact that a Royal Charter was granted in 1105 by Henry I to the monks of Tavistock allowing them to set up and run a weekly market. Two versions of the arms have been noted, one depicting a red and blue shield with two gold fleur-de-lis and one gold lion the other, as recorded in *Debrett's House of Commons,* showing just one fleur-de-lis. Both, however, include a fleece representing the town's woollen industry. Textiles did much to boost Tavistock's economy that when the church of St Eustachius was rebuilt between 1350 and 1450 the designers included a 'Clothworkers' isle on the south side.

TEDDINGTON (Middlesex)

Teddington Urban District Council used the device of a swan in reference to the River Thames.

TEIGNMOUTH (Devonshire)

Much of Teignmouth's history seems to have been ignored by the designers of its seal. Records indicate that the town was maintaining a significant port by the early part of the fourteenth century, but the silting up of the harbour and later persistent raids by privateers from Flemish ports caused its trade to decline. Cod fishing in Newfoundland did much to boost the economy, but it would seem that smuggling and privateering was, for a time, Teignmouth's most popular source of employment. When Sheldon Bridge, with its thirty-four wooden arches, was opened in June 1827 it would go on record as the longest wooden bridge in England. An then came Isambard Kingdom Brunel's railway, worked by the atmospheric system and running along an embankment between the sea and cliffs. But here we have just a silver shield charged with a red saltire cross and four red fleur-de-lis. C Wilfrid Scott-Giles suggests that the design was influenced by the heraldry of the Dean and Chapter of Exeter.

TENTERDEN (Kent)

The common seal dates from the time of Henry VI and as a member of the Cinque Ports the obverse displays a ship at sea. Gale Pedrick describes the vessel as a warship with a castle at the stern and a circular crow's-nest. The mainsail is charged with the arms of the Cinque Ports, while on the poop deck is flown the flag of St George. In the crow's-nest are three spears. In the sky can be seen a crescent and a sun. The reverse of the seal has a representation of St Mildred, the patron saint of the town church. Below the saint is a shield charged with a diagonal line (a bend) bearing three stars between the heads of four lions. These were the arms of the Pillesden family (one of would become Tenterden's first bailiff) which held the local manor. These can be seen again in the town arms, this time on the ship's mizzen sail.

TEWKESBURY (Gloucestershire)

It was here that Edward IV in 1417 defeated the Lancastrians and a notable Norman abbey built which managed to escape the Dissolution of Monasteries by King Henry VIII. The building was once noted as having the largest Norman tower in the country, its wooden spire contributing to an overall height of 260 feet. This, however, was lost during a storm on Easter Monday 1559. Pinnacles and battlements were added in 1660. This might have been a strong contender for inclusion in the town's heraldry, but Tewkesbury's seal is described as having a castle.

THAXTED (Essex)

The arms of this once Saxon settlement are described as having on a red ground two silver swords in saltire with, between the blades, a silver rose within a gold fetterlock. The rose and fetterlock are Yorkist badges and may refer to the fact that the manor in part had passed by inheritance to the House of York.

Cecelia, who was the mother of Edward IV, was made a gift for life of the property by her son Richard III. Wool once played an important contribution to the development of Thaxted as one of the most prosperous towns in Essex. But it was also known for its production of cutlery and this explains the crossed swords on a red ground which come directly from London's Worshipful Company of Cutlers.

THETFORD (Norfolk)

The town's seal shows a three-towered castle, the central and largest of which has a flag flying. On the other two smaller towers stand men, one holding a sword, the other blowing a horn. To the south-east of the town stands Castle Hill, but other than a mound, there is no trace of the Norman structure that once stood there.

THORNABY-ON-TEES (Yorkshire)

As the Battle of Hastings was in full flight, Robert I de Brus took a number of men over to Cleveland which was subsequently occupied. Pleased with the result, William the Conqueror gave him control of the land in the area which included Thornaby. It is the blue lion of the de Brus heraldry that we see in the centre of the shield. Also in the arms granted in 1893 we see references to the sixteenth-century Robert de Thormodbi who promised that if he survived the wounds received at Acre during the Crusades, would set up a shrine to the Virgin Mary at Thornaby's St Peter's Church. The ship and anchors forming the crest are in reference to a once-thriving maritime industry.

TIVERTON (Devonshire)

A Royalist stronghold during the Civil War, Tiverton Castle was besieged by Parliamentary troops who put to work their artillery from close by Shrink Hills. A lucky shot, it is said, hit one of the chains holding up the drawbridge which quickly fell, allowing Fairfax's roundheads into the castle. The siege over almost before it had begun, the Parliamentarians systematically destroyed much of the structure. Here in the town's seal we see a representation of Tiverton Castle together with its neighbour, St Peter's Church which dates from 1073. Below this is a row of Tiverton houses, two bridges over the River Exe, and a woolpack representing the woollen trade once so important to the population.

TODMORDEN (Yorkshire)

The town stands of the Calder which once marked the boundary between Yorkshire and Lancaster, the blue wavy line running through the centre of the shield is in reference to that river. The roses, one red, one white, recall the division. Dominating the Calder Valley and the town of Todmorden is the monument known as Stoodley Pike, designed in 1854 by local architect James Green. It replaced an earlier structure which was completed in 1815 to commemorate the defeat of Napoleon. Here we see it as a crest in the arms granted on 31 December 1896. Also here are a shuttle and spindle in reference to the woollen textiles industry which, thanks to the strong Pennine streams and local rivers that powered the machine looms, brought prosperity to the town.

TONBRIDGE (Kent)

The urban district council arms show a ship beneath an arched bridge and the motto *'Salus populi suprema lex'* which translates as The welfare of the people is the highest law.

TORQUAY (Devonshire)

During the Napoleonic wars Torbay was used as an anchorage for the Channel Fleet. This brought visiting relatives of the seamen whose liking for the place and its mild climate did much to promote Torquay as a pleasure and health resort. The motto translates as 'Health and Happiness'. Also in the arms granted in May 1893 are two white wings with, between them, a representation of a castellated gateway. Could this be in reference to Tore Abbey, founded at Torquay in 1196 as a monastery for Premonstratensian canons? Another indication of the town's association with the sea and ships is the gull and anchors crest.

TOTNES (Devonshire)

Recorded by the Heralds in 1560 as the arms of Totnes was a black shield charged with a silver castle on water between two silver keys. Totnes was fortified by King Edward the Elder in around 907, the construction of a castle, it is generally thought, to have been the work of Juhel of Totnes who had been given lands by William the Conqueror. But upsetting William II as he did, he was deprived of his property in around 1088 or 1089.

TREGONY (Cornwall)

Burke's *General Armory* gives, for the town, a pomegranate and a crest of a Cornish chough's head and neck in black holding a chaplet in its beak. The College of Arms notes the same, but with no reference to colours or the crest. Could it be that the pomegranate was in reference to the Norman family of Pomeroy whose castle once stood in Tregony and who built an early church in the town?

TRURO (Cornwall)

By the beginning of the fourteenth century Truro had become an important and safe port and was enjoying great prosperity from the fishing industry. So important that the arms granted in 1573 were charged with a ship and not one, but two fish. But there would soon be a new role in the form of tin and copper, the town becoming a 'Stannary town' for the purpose of stamping the metals from the Cornish mines. When supporters were authorised in 1877 what better choice could there be than a tin miner and fisherman.

TUNBRIDGE WELLS (Kent)

The heraldic symbol for a spring is a circle of silver and blue wavy lines, the arms granted to the town in 1889 having three of them, two on the shield, one in the arms of the lion that forms the crest. In 1606 Dudley, Lord North, while lodging close by discovered a spring which he was given to understand gave out water of healing properties. He had not been well and, having drunk from the spring, found that he was indeed feeling much better. He spread the word and soon tourists, including royalty, were drawn to the place by the thousand. In the drops placed on the red ground we have more water, the lion reminding all that the prefix 'Royal' was added to the name of the town in 1909.

TUNSTALL (Staffordshire)

Records show that iron and coal were being mined as far back as 1282, but it would be from the town's potteries that Tunstall would make its name. In its arms we see a soup tureen and a vase in memory of this important industry. There are also scythes for agriculture, two furnaces representing iron production and a Stafford Knot.

TWICKENHAM (Middlesex)

The College of Arms granted Twickenham its arms on 30 October 1913. The green Y-shaped division of the shield, according to C Wilfrid Scott-Giles, is not only symbolic of the town's name ('the place where the two ways meet'), but a reference to its historical connection with the See of Canterbury which has a similar shape in its heraldry. The antique lamp seen at the top of the shield is said to represent Twickenham's interest in literature, the arts and sciences via distinguished people from the town: the portrait painter Sir Godfrey Kneller (1646-1723), poet Alexander Pope (1688-1744), artist J W Turner (1775-1851) and the garden designer Batty Langley (1696-1751) to name but a few. There are crossed swords to represent a connection with the City of London and three red roses from the arms of William of Wykeham who built the tower of St Mary's Parish Church. Twickenham is on the River Thames, this represented in the crest by the swan on water. The swan grasps in its beak an eel which not only refers to the former lamprey fishing industry of Twickenham, but the local popular music venue of Eel Pie Island.

TYLDESLEY-WITH-SHAKERLEY (Lancashire)

The urban district council used the arms and crest of the Tyldesley family, a red chevron between three hillocks. The crest shows a gold pelican feeding its young with blood drawn from its own breast.

TYNEMOUTH (Northumberland)

Important to the town was its mining and sea trade, the supporters and ship crest representing this. The three crowns are from the Priory of Tynemouth and are said to represent the three important kings associated with the town: Edwin, the King of Northumbria who founded the priory around which the town grew, Oswald who rebuilt the town in 634 and Oswin who was buried in the Priory in 651 and became Tynemouth's patron saint.

UCKFIELD (Sussex)

The urban district council used the six martlets from the arms of Sussex.

UTTOXETER (Staffordshire)

On the seal, a shield charged with a Stafford Knot, fleur-de-lis, the word *Floreat* and the date 1896.

UXBRIDGE (Middlesex)

There in Old Windsor Street we see the Spotted Dog, with its Sedgwick Ales, and St Margaret's Church which has stood since at least 1245. Here too in the Edwardian postcard illustrated is the town's seal which displays three red piles within a black border charged with eight gold roundels. This device is taken from the arms of the onetime wealthy Uxbridge landowner, Basset of Welden.

VENTNOR (Isle of Wight)

Adopted in 1890 to promote Ventnor as a health resort, the town assumed a representation of Hygeia, the ancient Greek goddess of health, cleanliness and hygiene. There are roses too which are in reference to the Isle of Wight having been christened the 'Garden Isle'.

WAKEFIELD (Yorkshire)

C Wilfrid Scott-Giles includes in his *Civic Heraldry of England and Wales* details referring to the origins of Wakefield's arms, a gold fleur-de-lis on a blue ground, which he had received from the town clerk. It seems that permission to use the device was granted by Henrietta of France, queen of Charles I, who, having returned from France with part of her crown jewels, was hounded on her journey by Cromwell's men. At one time the house where she was staying was bombarded by the Roundheads and, fleeing from the scene, ended up sleeping in a ditch. But legend has it that at Wakefield she was well treated and in gratitude she asked that the fleur-de-lis should be used as the arms of the town. But other sources place the use of the emblem of France much earlier, one pointing out that these arms have been noted on a carved wooden boss on the roof of Wakefield Cathedral, giving it a date of not later than 1470. Another theory draws on the connection with Edmund of Langley who was given the Manor of Wakefield by his father Edward III. Edmund, the Duke of York, bore the Royal Arms of France and England and it is thought that the town may have used a single fleur-de-lis from this source. Returning to C Wilfrid Scott-Giles, he also mentions that upon its incorporation in 1848, Wakefield assumed arms consisting of representations of the Corn Market, Cattle Market and a sheaf of wheat.

WALLASEY (Cheshire)

As shipping ports go, Liverpool would probably come out on top. But in the Middle Ages Wallasey came a close second, some say even superior to the Lancashire hive of import and export. Hence the ship as the main charge of the Wallasey arms, the illustration being from a 1949 image by Paxton Chadwick. Here too on a blue ground are the three garbs from the arms of Chester and a bugle-horn. The latter is The Horn of Wirral which represents the ancient custom whereas Lords of the Manor required their tenants to sound a horn giving notice of enemy raids. For a crest, the dolphin and trident are suitable for such an important maritime borough. 'We are bold whilst we are cautious' reads the motto.

WALLINGFORD (Berkshire)

Gale Pedrick's superb book on borough seals illustrates the town seal which shows the figure of a king in armour and with sword in hand. A shield bearing the Royal Arms is carried, the helmet having a lion of England crest. Over the horse's neck is the letter 'E' and under it the letter 'H'. The horse is being ridden over a ford which alludes to the name of the town. In reference to the fifteenth-century seal, C Wilfrid Scott-Giles notes that the mounted figure generally resembles that of Edward IV on his Great Seal and goes on to suggest the letter 'H' was added during 1470-1 when Edward's reign was interrupted by the return of Henry VI. In a newspaper report covering the acceptance of letters patent of the new arms granted in August 1955, a Doctor Wilson announced that he was surprised some four years ago to learn that the portcullis 'used by Wallingford as its crest since 1640' had never been registered with the College of Heralds.

WALLSEND (Northumberland)

Hadrian's Wall had to end somewhere and where it did took on the name of Wallsend. Granted in 1902, the arms comprise a black shield charged with a gold Roman Eagle standing on, of course, a wall. Much of Wallsend's prosperity was in the mining of coal, represented by the black ground, and records show that between 1767 and 1825 some 209 deaths occurred as a result of pit accidents. One, a gas explosion on 18 June 1835, claimed the lives of 102 miners. There was also a copper-smelting industry which is represented in the arms by a sprinkling of gold drops. The motto tells how Wallsend arose on the site of the Roman fort of Segedunum.

WALSALL (Staffordshire)

A Corporation seal of the fifteenth century bears the Royal Arms flanked by two seated ions with their backs to the shield. Illustrated is the seal device with the addition of the Bear and Ragged Staff of Richard Neville, Earl of Warwick ('the Kingmaker') who held the Manor of Walsall in the fifteenth century. Note also the inclusion of the Stafford Knot at the bottom.

WALTON-UPON-THAMES (Surrey)

Situated on the right bank of the river, the town arms display a swan.

WANDSWORTH (London)

The five parishes, namely Clapham, Putney, Streatham, Tooting and Wandsworth that make up this London borough are represented by the five gold stars on the lower portion of the shield. Above this the Warennes, Earls of Surrey, are remembered by the blue and gold chequered pattern which has been charged with blue drops representing tears. Many of the persecuted French Huguenots (the 'unhappy Huguenots') settled in the Wandsworth area and the tears are theirs. Notice how the shield is divided by a line resembling a jig-saw. This is referred to in heraldry as 'nebuly' and was included in the arms granted to the borough on 6 July 1901 to represent the two rivers associated with Wandsworth, the Thames and Wandle. The red crosses around the shield are there to mark a connection of the borough with London, the representation of a Viking ship to recall the Danish invader that in the ninth century is credited with having sailed up the Thames as far as Putney.

WAREHAM (Dorsetshire)

On a red shield, three fleur-de-lis, a crescent and star all in gold. It will be noticed that the fleur-de-lis have been placed upside-down; C Wilfrid Scott-Giles explains this as being possibly an error on the part of the engraver who worked on the old seal. But more interesting is the tradition in Wareham that the reversal of the Royal associated symbol was ordered by Queen Elizabeth I as a mark of her displeasure after bells were not rung when she once passed through the town.

WARMINSTER (Wiltshire)

Based on an ancient seal, the arms adopted by Warminster Urban District Council show a mounted man in armour who is thought to represent Mordaunt, the first Lord of the Manor of Warminster.

WARRINGTON (Lancashire)

The eight gold-covered cups situated around the blue border of the shield and the unicorn in the crest are from the heraldry of the Boteler family, one-time holders of the manor and barony. The unicorn holds a banner charged with the red rose of Lancaster and a wheatsheaf of the Earldom of Cheshire in reference to the borough being situated on the borders of Lancashire and Cheshire. The lions on their ermine background are from Paganus de Vilars, the first Lord of Warrington. 'God giveth the increase', translates the motto. Warrington's arms were granted in May 1897.

WARWICK (Warwickshire)

The seal of the Corporation of Warwick illustrated and described by A C Fox-Davies shows a castle of three towers, the middle of which bears a shield charged with a ragged staff. Standing on each of the outer towers, watchmen can be seen blowing horns. In the sky, to the left there is a star and to the right a crescent moon. Turning now to C Wilfrid Scott-Giles and his 1933 edition of *Civic Heraldry of England & Wales,* we find a description more or less the same as the previous authority, but with the exception that the shield on the central tower is described as having three crosses from the arms of Beauchamp, Earls of Warwick, and the chevron and check pattern of Newburgh, also one-time Earls of Warwick. The sky devices, this time, are given as a sun between two stars and moon between two stars. Debrett's *House of Commons and The Judicial Bench* show this. Chris J Smith, a third reliable source, refers to the castle structure as 'a walled town' and points out that the seal design appeared in somewhat differing versions up to the time when arms were granted in 1930.

WARWICKSHIRE

Chris J Smith in his 1973 booklet *The Civic Heraldry of Warwickshire* notes how the bear and ragged staff is an emblem long associated with Warwickshire. Originally two separate devices, he suggests that there can be little doubt that both the bear and staff were unknown in the county before the time of the Beauchamps, the inheritors of the Earldom of Warwick in 1268. The county at first made no use of the device, its corporation seal showing, notes Mr Smith, '…the crowned face of an animal which some asserted was a bear, but which was in fact more like that of an heraldic lion.' But we must consider here the 1st Militia Regiment associated with the county who adopted the bear and ragged staff device as a headdress badge prior to 1881. It was also used as a collar badge for a short time by the Royal Warwickshire Regiment and its affiliated cadet corps (illustrated) at Rugby School.

WASHINGTON (Durham)

Three red stars and two red bars, the arms adopted by the urban district council are thought to have been devised in reference to the flag of the United States of America.

WEDNESBURY (Staffordshire)

Certainly the main sources of employment in Wednesbury were provided by its coal pits, iron production and the manufacture of nails. Recognition of this can be seen in the arms illustrated by the two black diamonds (the heraldic symbol for coal) and the blazing tower charged with the symbol for Mars (Mars the planet, not the god, of course) which is associated with iron. Henry II bestowed the Manor of

Wednesbury upon the Heronville family and it is from their heraldry that the silver lion with gold crown was taken. The arms were officially granted in 1904, but they were in use for a number of years prior to that. Regarding the flaming tower crest, another source states that this had been taken from the arms of Joseph Hopkins who as a local ironmaster had provided much charity to Wednesbury.

WEDNESFIELD (Staffordshire)

The battle scene depicted on the seal of Wednesfield Urban District Council is in reference to the Battle of Wodensfield which saw the Anglo Saxons defeated by the Danes of Northumberland on the field of Woden (now Wednesfield) on 4 and 5 August 910.

WELLS (Somersetshire)

From the Mendip Hills streams find their way down to the city and emerge at several places, in particular St Andrew's Well in the grounds of the Bishop's Palace. The water fills the moat around the palace and then spreads fertility in all directions. Based on an old seal, the arms show three wells and an ash tree, all symbols of the great gift from the Mendips. 'Wealth drawn from the spring flows forth unto our country and our people', translates the motto.

WENLOCK (Shropshire)

An ancient seal of Wenlock shows three canopied niches above three round-headed arches. In the centre is a representation of the Holy Trinity, on one side St Michael doing battle with the dragon, the other showing St Milburga, daughter of Merwald King of Mercia, holding a book in one hand and a pastoral staff in the other while a lamb sits at her feet. Three shields are placed below the niches, that in the centre belonging to Roger Montgomery, founder of the priory and benefactor of the town. The arms to the right are those of the Wenlock family and to the hart on the left is thought to be in reference to Edward IV. The Holy Trinity are patrons of the parish church. Also on record is another seal which in reference to the town's name shows a lock and the letters 'WEN'.

WEST BROMWICH (Staffordshire)

Except for the millrinds, records C Wilfrid Scott-Giles, all the charges on the West Bromwich arms granted in 1882 are from the heraldry of the Earls of Dartmouth who were seated at Sandwell Hall until 1855. This was the Legge family who were important landowners and industrialists in West Bromwich. Millrinds, the three devices accompanying the stag's head in the centre of the shield, are the iron work fixed to the middle of a mill stone on which it rotates. In heraldry though, the device is used to symbolise industry, coal and the production of springs, guns and nails being important sources of employment at West Bromwich. 'Work overcomes all difficulties', translates the motto.

WEST HAM (Essex)

Granted in 1887, the West Ham arms show in the centre on an ermine ground, a gold crozier representing Stratford Langthorne Abbey which once held the manor. By a charter dated 25 July 1135, William de Montfichet had granted the monks the land and it is the three chevrons from his heraldry that we see here (the colours having been reversed from gold chevrons on red). C Wilfrid Scott-Giles states that the ship and crossed hammers are in reference to local docks and industry. J H F Brabner's 1889 *Comprehensive Gazetteer of England and Wales* notes that at that time the industries of the borough included works for the manufacture of railway plant belonging to the Great Eastern Railway which covered an area of fifty-two acres and provided employment for some 5,000 people. Who would not be familiar with the crossed hammers insignia of West Ham United Football Club which had its origins in the Thames Ironworks and Shipping Company? There was, of course, a settlement in the area named Ham which appeared in the 1086 Doomsday Book as Hame. From the Old English, the word means a dry area of land between rivers or marshland, the settlement being located within boundaries of the rivers Lea, Thames and Roding.

WEST HARTLEPOOL (Durham)

Harts, anchors, a ship, gull or cormorant and the motto 'From the sea and from industry' tell in the town's arms much of its history. A representation of a hart in a pool and with a deerhound springing onto its back featured in a thirteenth-century seal of Hartlepool. Records show that by the early nineteenth century the town's port was on the decline so in 1823 it was decided that some form of new industry was required. A railway was built which opened the way for coal from the Durham coalfields that could be brought in and exported.

WESTBURY (Wiltshire)

Burke's *General Armoury* describes the arms of Westbury as a shield divided into gold and blue quarters with a cross and border made up of twenty lions. C Wilfrid Scott-Giles notes that the lions were probably included to denote that the manor was held by the Crown at the time of the Doomsday survey and that the cross represents the Paveley family who were granted the manor by Henry II.

WESTMINSTER (London)

Arms were granted to the city on 1 October 1601 which show a chained portcullis, two roses and a cross surrounded by five martlets. A portcullis and roses crest and lion supporters did not arrive until 1902. The arms, notes C Wilfrid Scot-Giles, are made up of the emblems of two monarchs particularly associated with Westminster Abbey: Edward the Confessor, who was responsible for the establishment of Westminster Abbey, and Henry VII who added the chapel that bears his name. Roses are included in the arms, representing the Tudor dynasty who raised Westminster to city status and established a palace there. The cross and martlets are from the heraldry of King Edward the Confessor. Sir William Cecil was the city's first Lord High Steward and it is his ermined lions that act as supporters. 'Oh Lord watch over the city', translates the motto.

WEYMOUTH AND MELCOMBE REGIS (Dorsetshire)

The boroughs of Weymouth and Melcombe were united in 1571, arms of a ship bearing two banners and a shield being granted just over twenty years after that. It has been a popular seaside resort since the Duke of Gloucester favoured the place in the 1780s, the ship at sea symbolizing this. Of the three heraldic charges we see the three lions of England, recalling that it was Edward I that gave Melcombe Regis its first charter. Eleanor of Castile, his wife, held the manor and she is represented by the lion and castle banner displayed from the mizzen. The chevrons on the shield are those of Gilbert de Clare, Earl of Gloucester, holder of the manor of Weymouth during the thirteenth century.

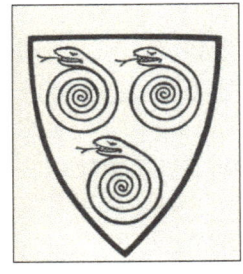

WHITBY (Yorkshire)

St Hilda founded Whitby Abbey in 657 where she remained until her death twenty-three years later. Legend has it that when stones of a circular shape were found at Whitby they were thought to be poisonous reptiles petrified by the prayers of St Hilda. But it would seem that the stones were in fact ammonite fossils upon which snake heads were carved by local artisans in support of the story. A shield charged with three coiled serpents became the heraldry of St Hilda. And in Whitby, prior to a grant of arms in 1935, the same device was used above which was placed a ship, mitre and a crozier. Ammonites or snakes; illustrators of the Whitby arms use either.

WHITEHAVEN (Cumberland)

In a Whitehaven seal the designer has chosen to illustrate the town's importance as a port by showing a ship passing the stone pier and lighthouse built by Sir Christopher Lowther in 1630. Prosperity grew in Whitehaven thanks to a busy tobacco import trade. Development of the port and a local mining industry was also due to the ingenuity of Sir Christopher. We can see a representation of the coal mine by the buildings and outhouses at its entrance depicted in the right-hand shield. The coal required transportation to its customers and it would be the railway that provided the means for this. See in the upper section of the seal an early locomotive hauling a train of eight coal trucks. Arms, however, were granted in 1894 and, in gratitude to the Lowther family, making use from their heraldry of the crest and shield of six black rings on a gold ground. The silver border and motto 'Let discord be absent from council' were the choice of the corporation.

WIDNES (Lancashire)

Arms were granted to Widnes on 5 June 1893 and these would not only represent the town's great industrial achievement by the inclusion of golden beehives and bees, but its speciality of alkali and soap manufacture. It would be John Hutchinson that built his first alkali factory in 1847 by the town's Sankey Canal. But as the amount of chemical works grew, so did the pollution resulting in it being referred to in 1888 as 'the dirtiest, ugliest and most depressing town in England.' In 1905 it had become 'a poisonous hell town.' A representation of a furnace and an alembic, used for distilling, form the crest, the motto translating as 'Industry enriches'. Red roses, of course, for Lancaster.

WIGAN (Lancashire)

The W D & H O Wills cigarette card illustrated shows a representation of the town's seal. It is generally thought that the building represents a town hall and the cross in front, a market cross.

WILTON (Wiltshire)

The town's fourteenth-century seal depicts a representation of the shrine of St Edith of Wilton who was the daughter of Edgar. Edith was educated by the nuns of Wilton Abbey where her body lies. It is said that St Dunstan attended a Mass at Wilton and was seen to be weeping. When asked why, he replied that he was weeping because he knew that Edith would die in three weeks. His prediction was correct, Edith dying on 15 September 984. The illustration is from Debrett's *House of Commons* and shows a representation of St Edith's shrine. Above is an angel bearing a shield charged with the three lions of England and below, the figure of a kneeling nun.

WILTSHIRE

A C Fox-Davies notes that the county has no armorial bearings and that 'The arms either of the City or See of Salisbury have done duty in their turn.' He also mentions in 1933 that the present seal of the county council depicts a view of Stonehenge.

WIMBLEDON (Surrey)

Arms were granted to the borough in 1906 which show a two-headed eagle charged on the right wing with a golden rose and on the left with a golden fret. The crest has a wheatsheaf supported by two Cornish choughs, the motto translating as 'Honour without strain'. On Wimbledon Common you will find both Caesar's Well and Caesar's Camp, the double-headed eagle being from the Roman politician and general's heraldry. The rose is a badge of Edward I, the fret that from the arms of Merton Priory, the choughs that of Thomas Cromwell who was once Lord of Wimbledon. The wheatsheaf is a reminder of Wimbledon's rural past, the gold and blue border around the shield representing the De Warennes who were the Earls of Surrey.

WINCHELSEA (Sussex)

An ancient seal is on record which shows a ship with a castle at the head and another at the stern. Also depicted is a shield bearing the three lions of England, two men blowing horns, four more hauling away at ropes whilst another is climbing the rigging. An eighth crew member can be seen acting as a steersman and directing the vessel using a side rudder. There is a star and crescent moon in the sky. Gale Pedrick reminds us that Winchelsea was once a member of the Cinque Ports and a principle point of embarkation for France. But, he noted in 1904, the town has been 'reduced' to an inland village two miles distant from the sea. There is a reverse to the seal depicting towers above several niches and houses over water to represent the town. On one embattled tower can be seen the half-length figure of a watchman bearing a lantern and, below this, a representation of a seated saint with before him a suppliant with hands raised and another holding a palm branch. In the niches we see a representation of the martyrdom of St Thomas á Becket. A bird sits on a spire looking across to a shield charged with the three lions of England. The arms of the town were as those of the Cinque Ports.

WINCHESTER (Hampshire)

On a red shield, five silver castles and two gold lions. Much in the lions is to do with England as Winchester once stood evenly with London as capital of the kingdom. In ancient seals there had been other castles. In 1253 there was one with triple towers depicted, another dated 1283 had two and a lion in company with a bust of Edward I.

WINDSOR (Berkshire)

What other than a castle could feature in the heraldry of this royal residence. In the common seal which dates from the time of Edward I we see a castle of three towers between two shields, one charged with the three lions of England and the other, which is divided, with the three lions on the left, another on the right at the top and above, a castle. Gale Pedrick, in his magnificent *Borough Seals of the Gothic Period*, illustrates a second 'Mayoralty' seal which also shows a castle. Above is a stag's head, between the antlers of which there is a shield bearing the arms of France and England. There are also the initials 'W' and 'B' which stand for Windsor and Berkshire. The stag's head most likely alludes to the neighbouring royal forest. Also illustrated are the Windsor arms as depicted in an Edwardian postcard.

In the centre of the several badges worn by the King's Own Stafford Militia appears a castle-type structure complete with a flag flying from a single tower. A castle, not unusual as a device incorporated into a regimental badge in reference to its geographical association, but in the case of the King's Own this is not a fortification of any Staffordshire town. So impressed was he with the regiment's appearance and conduct after an inspection in 1797, King George III requested that the Staffordshire Militia be sent to Windsor to take up Royal duties. A comfortable billet indeed, not only for the year 1797, but again in 1799, 1800 and 1801. Early in 1803 the regiment was once again embodied and on 17 May was ordered to march for Windsor. Pleased with the regiment upon its appearance at Little Park, Windsor in the following year, the King announced that in future 'They shall be called my own.' Prior to this, the Staffordshire Militia had worn scarlet jackets with yellow facings, but now the King's Own Staffordshire Militia would wear scarlet with blue. The officers at the same time were entitled to assume the device of the round tower at Windsor Castle on their accoutrements. In 1881, when The King's Own became the 3rd Battalion of the South Staffordshire Regiment, the device was taken into use by the regular battalions.

WIRKSWORTH (Derbyshire)

The urban district council's shield had, on one side, a rose over a crown, from the Derbyshire County Council's arms, and on the other, a number of miners' tools representing local coalpits.

WISBECH (Cambridgeshire)

Dating back to the twelfth century, Wisbech's Parish Church of St Peter and St Paul has a free-standing bell tower and was described by Sir John Betjeman as being typical of an English town. Here we see the saints, Peter with one of his keys, Paul with his sword, in the corporation seal.

WITNEY (Oxfordshire)

The town seal illustrated shows the Holy Lamb between a crescent and star. Woollen blankets have been made at Witney since the Middle Ages, the town at one time having five factories producing for a world market.

WOKINGHAM (Berkshire)

The name of the town was apparently derived from a Saxon chieftain called Wocca who owned lands in the area. Wokingham for a while, however, became corrupted as Oakingham and in consequence a representation of an acorn with oak leaves found its way to the council's seal.

WOLVERHAMPTON (Staffordshire)

A C Fox-Davies, who did not suffer fools gladly when it came to heraldry, had this to say regarding the arms illustrated for Wolverhampton in his 1894 edition of *The Book of Public Arms*: 'Wolverhampton has no Armorial Bearings; but not content with the bogus escutcheon which has been perpetrated for it, it also displays two other escutcheons, one of Wessex, the other of Leveson-Gower.' He then goes on to include a description of the arms that was published in the *Municipal Year Book* and adds that 'it is too good a joke to be omitted; for such is heraldry when affected by ignorant amateurs.' The description that so amused Mr Fox-Davies is dated 1848 and gives the designer of the 'seal' as a Mr Alfred Hall Browne and it purpose being for the use of the Mayor, Aldermen and Burgesses of the Borough of Wolverhampton: 'The centre shield (devised for the Borough Arms) is sable, a chevron between two cressets argent filled with burning coals in chief, and the stone column of Wulfrunhamton in base proper, augmented with an inescutcheon azure, a saltire of the second for Mercia, a canton of St George for Windsor, charged with the key of St Peter or.' As we can see from the illustration, one of the beacons with its burning coals has been obscured by the St George's cross and St Peter's key. The pillar referred to is of Saxon origin and can be found in the churchyard of Wolverhampton's St Peter's Church. The left-hand shield shows a Saxon crown, a cross which possibly commemorates Wulfrun the sister of King Edgar who founded the religious house at Hamton, and four martlets. On the right there is a ducal crown, two crosses and laurel leaves which the description gives as being for 'Leveson-Gower'. Above the central shield and suggesting a crest is the civic mace and sword, Stafford Knot and a ducal crown which are described as badges. In the second illustration we see the seal as depicted in an Edwardian postcard.

Wolverhampton County Borough was granted arms in 1898 and as a third illustration shows, they were of a much simpler design. Here still is the old Saxon column, the cross, burning beacon and keys of St Peter. But new additions come in the form of an open book representing Wolverhampton Grammar School, a woolpack for the town's important wool industry and a padlock reminding us that at one time Wolverhampton locksmiths held the reputation of being the most ingenious in England.

WOMBWELL (Yorkshire)

The urban district council used the device of a silver unicorn's head from the arms of the Wombwell family.

WOODSTOCK (Oxfordshire)

A silver uprooted tree stump, three silver stag's heads and a silver border charged with eight green oak leaves. Heraldically the supporters are described as savages wreathed about the temple and loins with oak leaves and each bearing clubs. Oak again in the crest, 'The branching horns of the stag' for the motto. These were the arms as recorded at the Visitation of 1634. Much here in reference to the name (in Old English it meant a clearing in the woods) and the fact that Woodstock was once a royal forest. Edward III had the stump of a tree as one of his badges. The motto '*Ramosa cornua cervi*' was taken from Virgil and was in reference to the horns of a stag given to Diana as an offering.

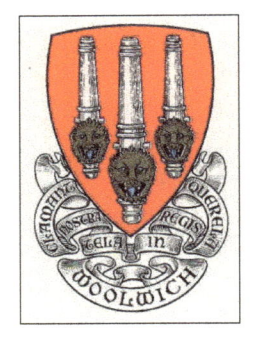

WOOLWICH (London)

Not surprisingly, the Borough of Woolwich in south-east London features three guns in its arms, their muzzles upwards, their breeches decorated with lion's faces, together with the motto '*Clamant nostra tela in Regis querela*' (Our weapons clash in the King's quarrel). The link obviously refers to the Royal Arsenal where the manufacture of armaments was carried out since the Board of Ordnance moved to Woolwich (The Warren in Tower Place) in 1671. Closure as a factory was in 1967, the Ministry of Defence finally moving out in 1994.

WORCESTER (Worcestershire)

Two coats of arms were recorded in the visitation books at the College of Arms which are described as 'the ancient and modern arms.' The ancient arms is divided into black and red quarters upon which is placed a silver tower of three turrets in reference to Worcester Castle. Black Worcester pears have been associated with the city since Roman times and three of these appear on the silver modern shield. A representation of the fruit was also used as a badge by the Worcestershire Yeomanry. The motto, 'Let the faithful city ever flourish', is one of three recalling Worcester's support of the Royalist cause during the Civil War. An ancient seal of the city shows a representation of Worcester Cathedral.

WORCESTERSHIRE

Without arms, the seal of the county displayed the pears of the City of Worcester.

WORKINGTON (Cumberland)

In the arms depicted in this Edwardian postcard we see a divided shield showing the heraldry of the Curwen family to the left and to the right, a representation of a blast furnace. The crest is the Curwen's too. The prosperity of the town owes much to its iron and steel production and its busy docks and sea trade.

WORTHING (Sussex)

Three fish swim in a sea of silver and blue. Above them is a cornucopia and a crest of a habited female figure holding a serpent. Below is a motto which explains all: '*Ex terra copiam e mari salutem*' (From the land plenty and from the sea health). The crest represents Hygeia, the ancient goddess of health. This was the coat of arms designed by Mr T R Hide in 1890 but were used without authority by this popular seaside resort until granted on 30 October 1919.

WOTTON-BASSETT (Wiltshire)

On a red ground, a silver chevron between three silver lozenges.

WYCOMBE (Buckinghamshire)

On a grassy mound a chained swan on a black ground.

YARMOUTH (Hampshire)

The town seal shows an ancient three-masted sailing ship.

YEOVIL (Somersetshire)

St John the Baptist is the patron saint of the town, the church bearing his name being known as the 'Lantern of the West' due to its high side isles and large windows. In the Yeovil seal we see St John between two trees and within a niche depicted holding the '*Agnus Dei*' on a plaque in his left hand and pointing to it with his right.

YORK (Yorkshire)

On a silver shield, five gold lions. The coat is often shown together with the civic sword and mace crossed behind the shield and with a chapeau above, as depicted in the Wills cigarette card illustrated.

YORKSHIRE

A C Fox-Davies points out that Yorkshire had no armorial bearings of its own but used those of the City of York. However, upon the formation of the county councils for the different ridings the West Riding simply assumed the design of the White Rose of York for its seal. The North Riding designed a coat which showed the Red Cross of St George on a silver ground with, above this, three white roses on a blue ground. The eagle with its wings spread of the East Riding seal is believed to have originated from a Roman standard.

BIBLIOGRAPHY

Benham, W Gurney: *Essex Borough & County Arms,* Benham & Co, Colchester, 1916.

Bretton, R: *West Riding Civic Heraldry,* Halifax Antiquarian Society, 1960.

Crosley, Richard: *London's Coats of Arms and the Stories They Tell,* Robert Scott, London, 1928

Debrett: *House of Commons and the Judicial Bench.* Dean & Son, London, several editions.

Fox-Davies, A C: *The Book of Public Arms,* T C & E C Jack, Edinburgh, 1894.

Fox-Davies, A C: *The Book of Public Arms,* T C & E C Jack, Edinburgh, 1915.

Ivall, D Endean: *Cornish Heraldry and Symbolism,* Dyllansow Truran, Redruth, 1988.

Lewis, John N C: *The Arms of Cheshire,* Kelvinator Ltd, 1949.

Pedrick, Gale: *Borough Seals of the Gothic Period,* J M Dent & Co, London, 1904.

Scott-Giles, C Wilfrid: *Civic Heraldry of England & Wales,* J M Dent & Sons, London, 1933.

Skidmore, Peter: *The Civic Heraldry of the Black Country,* The Black Country Society, 2003.

Smith, Chris J: *The Civic Heraldry of Warwickshire,* Coventry & Warwickshire History Pamphlets, 1973.

OTHER SOURCES

Civic Heraldry of England & Wales Website.

Heraldry of the World Website.

Ray Westlake Heraldry Archives.

Lightning Source UK Ltd.
Milton Keynes UK
UKHW052132091019
351302UK00005B/52/P